The Czartoryski Museum

Princess Izabela Czartoryska

The Czartoryski Museum

Adam Zamoyski

Azimuth Editions on behalf of
The Princes Czartoryski Foundation

Published in the United Kingdom
by Azimuth Editions on behalf of The Princes Czartoryski Foundation

The Princes Czartoryski Foundation
ul. Św. Jana 19
31–017 Kraków
Poland

Azimuth Editions
Unit 2a The Works, Colville Road
London W3 8BL, England

British Library Cataloguing in Publication Data
Data available

Library of Congress Cataloging in Publication Data
Data applied for

ISBN 1 898592 20 9

Photography: Christopher Phillips
Design: Anikst Associates
Printed in Great Britain by PJ Print, London

Cover illustration: *Lady with an Ermine*, by Leonardo da Vinci, probably the portrait of Cecilia Gallerani, painted ca. 1490

Frontispiece: Princess Izabela Czartoryska, by Richard Cosway, 1790

Contents

Foreword

To appreciate the Czartoryski Museum fully it is not enough to visit its galleries in the same way one does other museums. And to understand its true significance it is not enough to admire its major works of art. There are many other museums where one can find finer antiquities, better examples of medieval art, rarer objects and greater paintings – and ours is not the only Leonardo on earth. But there is no other museum with such an extraordinary story behind it, with such a personal character, and such a presence. To appreciate this, one should not merely look at the pictures, but read the text of this book.

The Museum, one of the first such institutions in the world, was founded by Princess Izabela Czartoryska, one of the most remarkable figures of her time. Her aim was to preserve the best of the past for the benefit of future generations. It was first and foremost Poland's past that she had in mind, and the story of the collection was tightly bound up with the continuing history of this country. The Museum was uprooted and dispersed more than once, it suffered from looting and political repression, and its survival hung in the balance several times. The happy ending of this dramatic story is due entirely to the extraordinary levels of devotion elicited in people of all kinds by the collection itself, with its highly personal character and its emotional appeal.

The museum cannot therefore be separated from the people whose endeavours and passions created, developed, cared for and defended it, and that means in the first instance my own forebears, who collectively devoted a vast amount of time and money to the enterprise over two hundred years.

Although I was born and brought up in Spain, in the bosom of the Spanish Royal Family, to which my mother belonged, I was keenly aware of this tradition and the emotions which had fired my Polish ancestors stirred within me too. When Poland regained her independence in 1989, I seized the chance to play my part in the continuing history of the museum.

I returned to the country from which my parents had been chased by war and communist repression, established my claim as the rightful owner of the Museum and Library, and created the Princes Czartoryski Foundation. My intention in doing so was and remains to guarantee the Museum's autonomous character and to provide it with a base on which it can continue to flourish and exert its curious, very personal appeal to a wider public.

Prince Adam Karol Czartoryski
Founder of the Princes Czartoryski Foundation

A book of 'Spiritual Reflections' belonging to Princess Zofia Czartoryska née Sieniawska, 1731

A Princess' Dream

The Dynasty

The princely rank of the Czartoryski family reaches back to the thirteenth century, when their forebears were rulers of the Grand Duchy of Lithuania. It was then a huge country whose sparsely inhabited expanses were of great strategic importance. In 1386 the reigning Grand Duke, Jogaila, married a Polish princess and became King Władysław Jagiełło, uniting the two countries and founding the royal dynasty of the Jagiellons, which was to rule the combined Polish-Lithuanian state for two centuries.

The junior branch of the ruling family became known by a name which derives from one of their main seats, Czartorysk in Volhynia. While their cousins reigned in Kraków, the Czartoryskis restricted their influence to this area, and it was not until the middle of the seventeenth century that they emerged from this comparative obscurity and began to play a significant part in the political life of the country as a whole.

And it was not until the end of that century that their slumbering royal ambitions were reawakened, with the arrival on the scene of Prince Kazimierz Czartoryski (1674–1741), Duke of Klewań and of Żuków, Castellan of Wilno, an intelligent and educated man with political ambitions. In 1693 he married Izabela Morsztyn, the lively daughter of Andrzej Morsztyn, who, as well as being Grand Treasurer of Poland, was also a noted poet. Together, these two built up the kernel of a political faction which came to be known as the *Familia*, 'the Family' – not surprisingly, since it was carried on jointly by their children Michał, August, Teodor and Konstancja.

Michał (1696–1775) rose to the rank of Chancellor of Lithuania, and married his daughter Antonina to Jan Jerzy Flemming, the immensely wealthy Treasurer of Lithuania – a match that would produce Izabela, founder of the Museum. His brother August (1697–1782), Palatine of Ruthenia, concentrated on building up the *Familia*'s financial base. In 1731 he married Zofia Sieniawska, the heiress to two enormous fortunes. He husbanded this wealth wisely and his two principal residences, at Puławy on the Vistula and Wilanów outside Warsaw, became centres of influence. In 1761 he married his son Adam Kazimierz to his niece, the daughter of Jan Jerzy Flemming, herself a great heiress, which ensured that in the next generation the Czartoryski fortune would be nonpareil. In 1720 their sister Konstancja added a valuable member to the family, by marrying Stanisław Poniatowski, one of the Swedish king Charles XII's

Family tree showing the main line of the Czartoryski family over the past three centuries

Kazimierz Czartoryski
Duke of Klewań and Żuków, 1674–1741
∞ 1693 Izabela Morsztyn

Fryderyk Michał
1696–1775
∞ 726 Eleonora Waldstein
1712–1795

August
1697–1782
∞ 1731 Zofia Sieniawska
1698–1771

Teodor
1704–1768
Bishop of Poznań

Konstancja
1700–1759
∞ Stanisław
Poniatowski

Ludwika
1733–1745
Prioress of the nuns of
the Visitation in Warsaw

Antonina
∞ Count Jerzy
Flemming

Adam Kazimierz
1734–1823
∞ 1761 Elżbieta (Izabela)
Flemming 1746–1835

Elżbieta
∞ Prince Stanisław
Lubomirski

Stanisław
Poniatowski
(King Stanisław II
Augustus)

Elżbieta (Izabela)
1746–1835
∞ Adam Kazimierz
Czartoryski

Teresa
1765–1780

Marya
1770–1854
∞ Prince Ludwig of
Württemberg

Adam Jerzy
1770–1861
∞ 1817 Princess
Anna Sapieha
1799–1863

Konstanty
1773–1860
∞ 1. 1802 Princess
Aniela Radziwiłł
∞ 2. 1821 Maria
Dzierżanowska

Zofia
1778–1837
∞ Count
Stanisław
Zamoyski

Witold
1824–1865
∞ Countess Marya
Grocholska

Władysław
1828–1894
∞ 1. 1855 Maria Amparo de
Munoz y Borbon, Countess of
Vista Allegre 1834–1864
∞ 2. 1872 Princess Marguerite
d'Orléans 1846–1893

Izabela
1830–1899
∞ Count Jan
Działyński

1

August
1858–1893
Duke of Vista
Allegre
Salesian Priest

2

Adam Ludwik
1872–1937
∞ 1901 Countess
Maria Ludwika
Krasińska
1883–1958

Witold
1876–1911

Małgorzata
1902–1929
∞ 1927 Prince
Gabriel de
Bourbon-Siciles

Elżbieta
1905–1989
∞ 1929 Count
Stefan
Zamoyski

Augustyn
1907–1946
∞ 1938 Princess
Dolores
de Borbon Orléans
1909–1996

Jolanta
1914–1987
∞ 1936 Prince
Władysław
Radziwiłł

Władysław
1918–1978
∞ 1949 Elizabeth
York

Teresa
1923–1967
∞ 1945 Jan
Groda-Kowalski

Ludwik
1927–1944

Adam Karol
1940

Ludwik Piotr
1945–1946

most brilliant generals, described by Voltaire as 'a man of extraordinary merit'.

The *Familia* worked like clockwork: Michał did the thinking, August provided the funds, their brother-in-law Stanisław Poniatowski took care of the execution while Teodor, who had become Bishop of Poznań, blessed the enterprise. By the 1750s they were the most powerful faction in Poland. And they were all of one mind in their determination to rescue the country from the economic decline and political anarchy into which it had subsided.

They decided to use the support of Russia, whose influence was dominant in Poland, to put one of their own on the Polish throne – either August's son Adam Kazimierz Czartoryski or Konstancja's son Stanisław Poniatowski. In the event, the new ruler of Russia, Catherine II, decided to back Poniatowski, who had been her lover several years before, and thus Michał's grandson was crowned king in 1764 under the name of Stanisław II Augustus.

But at this moment of ostensible triumph the political plans of the *Familia* began to go wrong. While the new king shared their vision of regenerating Poland under Russian protection, he was determined to do this in his own way. He ignored their warnings and defied Russia. Poland's other neighbours took advantage of this political crisis, which was only defused by Russia, Prussia and Austria carving great slices off the country in an act that has gone down in history as the first partition of Poland. Faced with the impossibility of political action, the Czartoryskis shifted their energies into other areas.

Prince Adam Kazimierz Czartoryski (1734–1823) had been groomed for great things from his very birth. He was carefully educated and then sent off on a foreign tour, but he was a disappointment to his father and uncle. He did not evade his perceived social obligations. He took an active part in the life of the Polish parliament, the Sejm, he held the office of Governor General of Podolia and a number of other posts. In 1765 he accepted command of the newly formed Cadet Corps, and he was active in the Commission for National Education, overseeing the production of school textbooks. But he was an intellectual rather than a fighter or a politician. He had a literary bent, which he indulged by writing plays, and he was interested in foreign languages, of which he spoke several – he even corresponded in Sanskrit with the great orientalist Sir William Jones. In his

Prince Adam Kazimierz Czartoryski, by Elisabeth Louise Vigée-Lebrun, 1793

A pastoral entertainment at Powązki, by Jean-Pierre Norblin de la Gourdaine, 1785

Warsaw residence, the Blue Palace, and at his country seat of Puławy, he gathered around him men of learning, writers and artists.

Adam Kazimierz was also something of a disappointment to his wife. Izabela (or Elżbieta as she was actually christened) was born in 1746, the only daughter of Jan Jerzy Flemming and Antonina Czartoryska. Her mother died while she was still a baby, and she was brought up by her grandmother, who made no attempt to provide her with an education. She married Adam Kazimierz at the age of fifteen, but the arranged marriage had taken no account of their characters. The bookish prince showed scant interest in his young bride, and ignored her in favour of his intellectual pursuits. This at least left Izabela free to amuse herself as best she could. She was not beautiful and she knew it, but she had great charm and knew how to please. As a result, she had no trouble in satisfying an enthusiastic taste for amorous adventure.

Princess Izabela also had a passion for travel, and she accompanied her husband on his journeys, sometimes dressed as a page if he could not accommodate the full equipage due to a lady of her rank. In 1768 they went to Saxony, Austria, France and England; in 1772 she went to Holland and England once more; the following year she was in Paris, where she called on the celebrated literary hostess Madame Geoffrin and met Jean Jacques Rousseau – whom she hardly dared talk to as she had not read any of his books. When she had met Benjamin Franklin the previous year, she became so tongue-tied that she burst into tears. But her lack of education did not hamper her in other quarters. She could empathise with Queen Marie Antoinette and had a passionate affair with the dashing Duc de Lauzun. The influence of these experiences did not take long to manifest itself.

On her return to Poland, Princess Izabela transformed her estate of Powązki just outside Warsaw into a sentimental rural retreat similar to the Trianon at Versailles. In a landscaped park with artifical grottos, cascades and temples dedicated to the gods of mythology, she erected for every member of her family and her principal courtiers castle ruins or thatched cottages whose interiors were appointed like luxurious palaces – one had a subterranean tiled bathroom reached by a mechanical lift. Nothing was what it appeared in this huge playground for the indulgence of hedonism: a gnarled old tree-trunk contained a boudoir, complete with silken couch. The remarkable thing about it was that it was all meticulously planned by herself, rather than being delegated to professionals. In the process she learned so much about the subject that she later wrote and published a book entitled *Various Thoughts on the Manner of Laying out Gardens*.

All this frivolity masked a gradual coming of age, as well as an improvement in relations with her husband. Motherhood turned out to be a defining experience, and Princess Izabela took to the role of parent with a warmth as well as a sense of duty rarely met with at the time. In 1780 she suffered a terrible blow, when her eldest daughter Teresa died engulfed in flames after a spark from a fireplace ignited her dress. Four years later she watched with dismay as her next daughter's arranged marriage, to Prince Ludwig of Württemberg, turned to violent abuse.

In 1789 Princess Izabela made another journey to England and Scotland, this time in the company of her son Adam Jerzy. This progress through a landscape redolent of the immensely popular poems of Ossian and drenched in the history of the newly fashionable Middle Ages was a landmark in her emotional development. She began to cast off the eighteenth-century sensibility of her youth with its rococo frivolity, and indulged a more spiritual and Romantic strain of thought. This coincided with a growing awareness of the perils threatening her own country.

In the late 1780s she had joined her husband in support of the 'Patriot' party formed by the younger generation of the *Familia*, which was agitating for immediate political reform. Taking advantage of Russia's temporary distraction by a war with Turkey, they prepared a progressive new constitution, which was passed on 3 May 1791. Princess Izabela returned to Poland just as the constitution was being enacted, and she set about commemorating the event in a fitting manner. Her court poet Dionizy Kniaźnin illustrated and defined the role she had arrogated for herself in a specially written play, *The Spartan Mother*, in which she played the leading role when it was staged in the court theatre at Puławy. Henceforth she poured all her energy and her feeling into the cause of her country. She assisted at military manoeuvres, encouraging the young officers and sending her own son Adam Jerzy to join their ranks, and wrote a patriotic marching-song for them. But the euphoria was quickly superseded by the gloomy realities of war.

Russia could not countenance the liberal constitution of 3 May 1791, and in 1792 Catherine II sent in her troops. Prince Adam Jerzy fought valiantly and won the cross of *Virtuti Militari* for his bravery at the battle of Granne, but defeat was unavoidable. The Prussians seized the opportunity to invade from the other side, and Poland lost more of her territory in the second partition that followed. She also lost what was left of her autonomy, as Russian troops remained on Polish soil and Catherine dictated policy.

Seeing no other means of national revival than armed struggle, Princess Izabela lent her support to a group of patriots led by the hero of the American Revolution, Tadeusz Kościuszko. In 1794 he launched an insurrection to expel the Russians from Poland. But despite some initial successes, the Poles were crushed by the combined armies of Russia and Prussia, and in 1795 the Polish state was finally carved up between her three neighbours and wiped off the map.

The Czartoryskis' involvement in these events had incurred the displeasure of Catherine of Russia, who ordered her troops to devastate Powązki and Puławy and to sequestrate all their lands. This confiscation was lifted only after their two sons, Adam Jerzy and Konstanty, were sent to the court at St Petersburg, in the guise of hostages.

A Shrine to the Nation

In 1796 Princess Izabela returned to Puławy, which presented a picture of ruin and desolation. The house had been looted and partly burned down, the park had been thoroughly vandalized. Never one to shirk a challenge, she began rebuilding, first the house itself, then the landscape park, with its numerous statues, its Chinese pavilion, its cascade, triumphal arch, grottos and bridges. But even as these were rising up anew from the devastation, she embarked on a quite different enterprise. It was the fulfilment of a personal dream of extraordinary ambition, one that had been taking shape in her thoughts over the past decade – to create in the midst of this Arcadian setting a kind of shrine, a national museum dedicated to preserving the memory of Poland's past and her place in history.

It was a revolutionary concept. Although people had been collecting precious and unusual objects from the beginning of time, the impulse had been either a fashion-led desire to embellish their homes or a quest for the wondrous and the rare. Such a collection came to be known as a *wunderkammer*, a chamber of marvels. During the Renaissance, a number of rulers and potentates built up collections supposed to facilitate study and this scientific approach led eventually to the foundation of the British Museum in 1753. The Polish king Stanisław Augustus, a connoisseur who had built up a remarkable private collection, and who had visited England the year after the foundation of the British Museum, had dreamed of creating a *Musaeum Polonicum* along similar lines.

The second half of the eighteenth century saw a revival of interest in antiquities of every kind. Much effort was devoted to recording the past, cataloguing monuments and listing objects of historical importance. In 1793, when the revolutionary mob had destroyed much of France's religious and royal treasures, the Convention hurriedly established the Musée Français as a repository in which to safeguard the surviving national heritage.

Princess Izabela's idea was far more ambitious, and far ahead of its time. She set out to preserve elements rescued from the foundering Polish ship of state, and to use them in the service of the national cause. Her intention was to recreate, through a careful selection and juxtaposition of objects, a coherent picture of the past on which to model a vision for the future. It was not until 1833, when king Louis Philippe began work on transforming the palace of Versailles into a monument to the past greatness of France, that anyone else took up her idea.

Princess Izabela's enterprise was circumscribed by her means and led entirely by her intuition, but both of these proved up to the mark. She had inherited the remarkably rich collection of the Sieniawskis, which included a magnificent array of Turkish trophies from the campaign of 1683. Her close relations with her cousin King Stanisław Augustus and with the prime aristocratic families of Poland, the Lubomirski, Zamoyski, Potocki, Sapieha and Radziwiłł, gave her access to an abundance of historical objects, and they were happy to let her pick out those she found most significant. With the support of the clergy she was able to acquire a number of captured banners that had been hung over the tomb of St Stanisław in the cathedral of Kraków's Wawel hill and even the stirrup of the Grand Vizier Kara Mustafa, left there as a votive offering by King Jan III Sobieski. She personally removed various fragments of royal sarcophagi, an assortment of stones and other elements from the ruins of the royal castle itself.

But none of this could satisfy her central need, which was for a core of objects associated with the Polish state itself, to act as the defining relic in her national shrine. What she needed was, as it were, the crown jewels. But that was a forlorn hope. The actual Crown Jewels had always been kept, along with a number of relics, trophies and treasures, in the royal castle on Wawel hill, alongside the coronation and funereal regalia held in the treasury of the Cathedral. In 1795 Prussian troops occupied the Wawel and looted the royal treasury, driven not only by lust for gold, but also by the intention of destroying the symbols of Polish statehood (the jewels were unpicked and melted down).

After the Prussians had gone, the distinguished antiquary Tadeusz Czacki painstakingly gathered up every object that had survived this disaster, even twisted or broken fragments. He also opened some of the royal tombs for examination and removed from them whatever relics he could find. He obtained permission from the Austrians, who were now the masters in Kraków, to take these away for safekeeping, along with other

Key to the Temple of the Sibyl, designed by Princess Izabela, 1801

mementoes and documents he had collected. When he learnt of what Princess Izabela was doing, he handed his collection over to her.

Princess Izabela had already decided exactly what form her national shrine was to take and how these objects were to be accommodated within it. What she wanted was a hall of memory, and as she intended to situate it in the sylvan setting of the park of Puławy, she naturally saw it in the form of a classical temple. As her model, she selected a half-ruined circular temple dating from the first century at Tivoli outside Rome. Princess Izabela had never been there, but the place drew foreign travellers and was well known from their accounts and through a number of prints and pictures. Among the many visitors to the place was the Polish architect Christian Piotr Aigner, who had been sent to study in Rome on a bursary provided by King Stanisław Augustus. He had taken detailed drawings of the circular temple, and had even made a scale model of it. After his return to Poland in 1782, Aigner worked for the king, for the army and for a number of private clients, developing an Italianate neoclassical style very much his own. He worked for Princess Izabela on various commissions, and it is probable that it was he who suggested the temple as a model for that in which she would house her museum.

There was more to the suggestion than just aesthetics, for the rotunda of Tivoli was pregnant with associations. It was thought, erroneously, to have been the seat of the Tiburtine Sibyl. The Sibylline cult, born in Asia Minor, venerated a Sibyl who was allegedly the daughter of Zeus and endowed with second sight. As the cult developed, Sibyls proliferated, with the most famous, at Delphi, Cumae and Tibur (Tivoli), being consulted as oracles. The books in which the Sibyl of Cumae had written down her prophecies were kept on the Capitol in Rome, and were believed to hold the key to the future of the Roman state. Thus the round temple of Tivoli was associated with clairvoyance and augury, which not only appealed to the imagination of Princess Izabela, but also fitted neatly with her concept, which was encapsulated in the motto which she would inscribe over the portals of her own shrine, *Przeszłość Przyszlosći* (The Past to the Future). She meant to take all that was best and most inspiring from the past and to lay it at the service of the future.

Princess Izabela began work on her temple in 1797, on an escarpment overlooking a backwater of the river Vistula. The temple sheltered among trees, and the surroundings

Three of the series of bronze panoplies commemorating great military commanders of the past which adorned the walls of the Temple of the Sibyl: those of Lew Sapieha, Stanisław Żółkiewski and Jan Zamoyski

were further enhanced by the scattering of a number of great boulders. The idea was to recreate the surroundings of the original, and thereby give the temple its own other-worldly, almost sacred space.

Aigner's building is almost twice the size of the temple at Tivoli. It has two large chambers, the lower one visible only from the side on which the ground falls away towards the Vistula. Thus the front of the temple represents only a single-storey domed rotunda ringed with eighteen Roman columns. The temple is approached up a flight of steps flanked by two granite lions donated by Tsar Alexander I after he had stayed at Puławy in 1805, and entered through an imposing portal surmounted by the inscription 'The Past to the Future'.

The key that opened the heavily studded double doors, a gilt-bronze replica of the staff of Hermes, entwined by two snakes and crowned by two wings topped with a pine-cone, was designed by Princess Izabela herself. As well as being the messenger of the Gods, Hermes was also a guide, and, more importantly, a link with the dead and protector of

The Temple of the Sibyl at Puławy, by Jean-Pierre Norblin de la Gourdaine, 1820 things found. The key was inscribed in Greek with the words *Mnemez Anoigo Hieron* ('I open the temple of memory'), and with Princess Izabela's initials and the date 1801, that of the museum's opening.

Once inside, the visitor found himself in an austere space with a somewhat sacral feel. The walls were finished in marblized stucco, the only architectural feature being a semi-circular arched niche opposite the entrance. The solemn atmosphere was enhanced by the slightly purplish tinge given to the natural light as it passed through the amethyst-tinted glass of the dome. And what he was subjected to next one can only describe as an experience, one designed to raise the spirits of a people who had just been defeated and humiliated.

The niche facing the entrance was partly veiled by a curtain of crimson velvet draped from a gilded halberd. Within, high on the wall of the niche was a panoply around King Jan III Sobieski's 'Augury Shield'. No object could have been more apposite to Princess Izabela's concept than this Renaissance shield depicting the Emperor Constantine's victory over Maxentius at the battle of the Milvian Bridge outside Rome in 312 AD, a triumph of Christian arms over paganism. The probably apocryphal story of the shield was that it had been found behind the miraculous picture of Christ in the Wawel Cathedral and presented to King Jan III just as he was setting off to do battle with the Turks besieging Vienna, where he was to command the last great victory of Christian arms over the infidel. Other elements in the panoply represented the greatest military victors in Polish history: King Władysław Jagiełło and Grand Duke Witold, who had crushed the might of the Teutonic Order at Grunwald in 1410, and King Stephen

Memorial casket containing a fragment of the skull of King Bolesław the Brave taken by Princess Izabela from his tomb in Poznań cathedral

Bathory, who had defeated the Muscovites. Below this, there was an arrangement of Polish armour and captured military accoutrements. The whole was a powerful statement of Poland's past military prowess.

The walls of the chamber were decorated with symbolic trophies representing the illustrious families of Poland: the Tenczyński, Lubomirski, Wiśniowiecki, Zamoyski, Sieniawski, Radziwiłł, Jabłonowski and so on, each a panoply incorporating the arms of the family in question with pieces of armour, swords, lances and batons of command. Either side of the niche stood clusters of old Polish banners, captured enemy standards, staffs of office and court halberds.

In front of the niche stood what was in effect the altar of the temple – the 'Royal Casket'. Made of black ebony with gold fittings, set with diamonds and lined with green velvet, the casket contained three removable trays. These contained several dozen small

One of the trays from the Royal Casket, containing assorted royal memorabilia

objects, including relics retrieved from the royal tombs at the Wawel, elements of jewellery, miniatures, prayer-books, crucifixes, pictures of saints, fragments of clothing, lace, watches and even buttons that had belonged to kings and queens of Poland. It was a symbolic re-creation of the vanished Crown Jewels.

The remainder of the exhibits in the main chamber of the temple were housed in two great mahogany cabinets with purpose-built glass-covered drawers. The cabinets were closed and the objects hidden from view. They would be revealed to the visitor by the guide – visiting the temple was not supposed to take the form of a gentle browse through works of art, it was a didactic experience orchestrated by the guide, who was usually Princess Izabela herself. The cabinets contained objets d'art associated with Polish kings, such as the coronation slippers of King Zygmunt II Augustus and the aigrette of King Stephen Bathory. These were complemented by rare books and incunabula, drawings and documents. There were also Polish militaria, many with emotive stories behind them. There was the sabre belonging to King Jan III which he had donated as a votive offering to the shrine of the Virgin at Loreto after his victory over the Turks at Chocim, which had been salvaged from Loreto in the 1790s by Polish soldiers serving under Bonaparte and offered to the temple in Puławy (only to be destroyed by German soldiers in 1939). There were Hetman Mikołaj Hieronim Sieniawski's spoils from the victory over the Turks at Vienna in 1683; Prince Józef Poniatowski's dolman and the bullet-torn jacket in which Colonel Kozietulski had led the famous charge of the Polish Chevau-Légers at Somosierra in Spain in 1808.

Along the top of the cabinets, Princess Izabela had placed a number of small urns and miniature sarcophagi containing physical relics of kings and great men of Poland, each adorned with an inscription in Latin and Polish. In front of the cabinets stood two great chests containing objects of significance to Polish statehood. One held a collection of privileges and charters of Poland's princes and kings, the other almost 1,700 gold, silver and copper coins. In front of the right-hand showcase stood an antique table said to have belonged to King Kazimierz the Great, and on it a small casket destined for visitors' offerings. These were not intended so much to help with the upkeep of the museum as to register the visitor's participation, his or her ex-voto.

Gothic Romance

Although the Temple of the Sibyl was concerned with the past and its significance for the future, the present could not be excluded entirely, particularly in the light of the dramatic changes taking place in Napoleonic Europe. The Czartoryskis were a very political family, fired by the wish to see their country reborn. Prince Adam Kazimierz saw the best chance of this through cooperation with Austria, while his son Adam Jerzy placed his hopes in Russia. A close friend of Alexander I, he even became Russia's Foreign Minister in 1801. Princess Izabela on the other hand looked to France.

After the failure of Kościuszko's insurrection in 1794, many young Poles had been obliged to flee abroad, and large numbers of them went to France, at whose side they hoped to carry on the armed struggle against the three powers which had partitioned Poland. In 1797 a Polish Legion was formed alongside the French army in Italy, under the command of General Jan Henryk Dąbrowski. It was intended as a spearhead of a new insurrection in Poland, but it never fulfilled this purpose.

The Gothic House at Puławy, by Wilibald Richter, ca. 1840

The hopes of the Francophile patriots were vindicated in 1807 when, following his victory over Prussia, Napoleon restored a small part of Poland to independence as the Duchy of Warsaw. In 1809 this went to war in support of Napoleon. The Polish army under Prince Józef Poniatowski defeated the Austrians and set off in pursuit. His road lay through Puławy, and Princess Izabela set out to greet the victorious troops as they approached. She choreographed a procession of people bearing trophies of past ages taken from the Temple of the Sibyl, whose key she carried herself and presented to Prince Józef. It was a momentous occasion, a landmark in her life and in that of her collection, for on that very day she opened a second unit of her museum, the 'Gothic House', whose wall appropriately bore the inscription: 'Henceforth let our victories efface the memory of the defeats we have suffered'.

The idea of the Gothic House had come to Princess Izabela while she was still building the Temple of the Sibyl, and sprang from the necessity of finding a place to exhibit the growing number of non-Polish memorabilia which were piling up at Puławy. Many had been acquired in the course of her travels, particularly in England and Scotland in 1790. In her travel journal she noted how her imagination was stirred by places haunted by memories of Celts and Romans, by 'Ossianic' legend, and how she relived medieval history in its authentic settings as she visited castles and gothic cathedrals. These sensations awoke in her a desire to gather pieces of this magical past, and she began to collect.

Among her first acquisitions were fragments of Shakespeare's chair, bought from his house in Stratford-on-Avon, as well as a carved powder-horn associated with Henry VIII and the death-mask of Oliver Cromwell, both purchased at auction in London. From the sister of Captain James Cook she bought the great explorer's cutlass. Various aristocrats presented her with paintings and pieces of armour, each with some romantic story attached to it. And Princess Izabela supplemented this

Bronze chair made ca. 1800 to accommodate the back and seat of Shakespeare's chair, purchased by Princess Izabela in Stratford-on-Avon in 1790

with more humble sentimental mementoes such as moss scraped from Stonehenge, wild flowers picked at the alleged tomb of Fingal, and suchlike.

These disparate objects were soon joined by others donated by her many friends all over Europe; when word got about that she was collecting things with historical associations, people amiably began sending her mementoes and curiosa they had stumbled on. As none of this could be made to fit the context of the Temple of the Sibyl, it would have to be exhibited in another building. After some thought, Princess Izabela decided that this should be in the 'Gothic' style. This was logical, since the impulse had first come from her discovery of gothic England. It also seemed to reflect most faithfully the essentially chivalric culture of the western European past to which many of the objects in question belonged.

Like the Temple of the Sibyl, the Gothic House was designed by Christian Piotr Aigner, but the guiding idea and all decisions on detail were the Princess' own. It was, in fact, anything but gothic in style – baroque columns and elements of classical decoration jostled with arched windows to produce a bizarre effect. The walls were rendered and painted to imitate brickwork, and broken up by windows of every shape, rosettes and even a frieze. The heterogeneous building was rendered even more curious by the outside walls being incrusted with fragments of stone taken from other buildings, metal relicts and memorial tablets. The visual jumble was accompanied by thematic confusion, with objects of Polish significance punctuated by foreign elements, such as the 'antique nail taken by Lord Elgin from a monument in Athens' and 'a bronze hand found on the shores of the Black Sea not far from Odessa'. There was 'a piece of stone from the castle of Fotheringay, where Mary Stuart was executed', fragments from Petrarch's house and from the castle in Moravia in which Richard the Lionheart had been held captive; a piece of Tadeusz Kościuszko's coffin and several cannon-balls from battlefields on which he had fought, with, thrown in for good measure, 'a nail from the ship named the Bellerophon, on which Napoleon was taken to St Helena'.

The inside of the building was no more consistent. Each of the six rooms was different in style and atmosphere. The oval chamber on the first floor lined with green silk was bright and airy, the downstairs rooms were plunged in a semi-religious gloom by the feeble light coming through the stained-glass windows. But whether they were light or gloomy, large or small, all of them were characterised by the same kind of promiscuity. The beam supporting the ceiling of the oval chamber on the ground floor was inscribed with the words: 'Tender recollection can rescue from oblivion all that fate has destroyed or time devoured'. And it was clear that Princess Izabela was in the business of rescuing whatever she could without much discrimination. The walls were covered with an embarrassment of unmatched objects of every kind and widely discrepant value, which also cluttered tables and filled cabinets, showcases, chests and caskets in a magnificently exuberant chaos of allusion.

The Gothic House was meant to embrace the whole of human experience. But it was to do this in a very particular way. Over the door was a grey marble plaque with a quotation from Virgil's Aeneid: *Sunt lacrimae rerum et mentem mortalia tangunt* (objects weep tears, and though dead can still arrest the heart). Her idea was to bring together objects endowed with sentimental significance which opened up possibilities for boundless historical and sentimental reflection on the glories and miseries of human life. One thing the collection was *not* meant to be was a centre of artistic or aesthetic

A group of objects associated with legendary pairs of lovers: fragments of the supposed grave of Romeo and Juliet in Verona; glass oval with relics of Abélard and Héloise; agate container with relics of Petrarch and Laura, acquired in Italy by Prince Adam Jerzy Czartoryski; 17th-century silver-gilt and enamelled cup containing the ashes of El Cid and Ximena.

study or interest. An artistically pleasing or precious piece was clearly an advantage, but the most important aspect of any item was that it be associated with people or events.

This kind of collection required explanation, and, being of a literary bent, the Princess saw to this herself. She produced catalogues which suggest and make connections, and whose perusal offers a fascinating glimpse of the European mind at this turning point between eighteenth-century rationalism and nineteenth-century Romanticism. The juxtaposition of the two buildings and their collections was in itself a remarkable record of the change that had taken place in the European sensibility. The Temple of the Sibyl symbolized classical purity, stylistic unity, and a concept both clear and divine. The Gothic House stood for a more tangled emotional approach, an eclectic and almost frenzied flight from rationality, and a shift from the worship of God to the glorification of

Man – as hero, as heroine, as doomed lover, vanquished warrior, captive ruler, as sage, genius and artist, but also as a community, in his national aspirations, his wars and his trials.

These trials often favoured her purpose. In France, she took advantage of the revolution's depredations to obtain a crystal hunting-flask associated with Francis I, some mementoes from the royal family's incarceration in the Temple prison and fragments taken from the royal necropolis at Saint Denis while it was being destroyed in 1793. She made contact with Alexandre Lenoir, who had in 1791 been appointed by the National Assembly to salvage works of art confiscated from the Church, and later founded the Musée des Monuments Français. From him she obtained the relics of Abélard and Héloise, which he had personally removed from a grave in the monastery of Le Paraclet in 1790

Key to the Gothic House, with an inscription taken from the *Aeneid* proclaiming that women lead in great works and provided with his certificate of authenticity. She also received a number of precious relics from the celebrated Baron Vivant Denon, who had taken part in Bonaparte's Egyptian campaign and achieved renown by his publication of the first major work of Egyptology. It was from him that she received the ashes of El Cid and Ximena, removed from a tomb in the cathedral of Burgos when it was ravaged by French troops in 1810.

Another who helped Princess Izabela was Jean Charles Beydaels de Zittaert, custodian of the Treasury of the Order of the Golden Fleece in Brussels. In 1789 Beydaels managed to absorb into this the finest pieces from the arsenal founded in the city by the Dukes of Brabant in the fifteenth century. In 1794, when the French victory at Fleurus exposed Brussels to the armies of revolutionary France, Beydaels evacuated the treasury. He presented to Princess Izabela thirty or so choice pieces from his collection, mainly portions of suits of armour, each one linked with a famous personage. Some of the connections were undoubtedly authentic, like the pieces of a suit of armour for knight and horse made ca. 1600 in Italy for Archduke Albrecht, governor of the Netherlands, or the elements of armour belonging to the Emperor Maximillian II. But other attributions were more far-fetched, linking objects with Philip the Good, Charles the Bold, the Emperor Charles V, and even Montezuma. There were also nine Spanish ship's standards supposed to have been flown at the Battle of Lepanto, which turned out to be of much later date.

The whole question of authenticity was of vital importance to Princess Izabela. Those things she had picked up herself she could vouch for – she actually describes stealing a quill pen from the desk of Frederick the Great while visiting Sanssouci. Others had been acquired by members of the family over the previous century directly from figures such as Charles XII and Peter the Great, with whom they had been in direct contact. The same was true of George Washington's teacup, donated by himself through the agency of the poet Julian Ursyn Niemcewicz. Problems arose with items sent in by others, who were eager to feed her desire to have objects of human interest. A fifteenth-century shield found in Switzerland was recorded as being from the First Crusade, a Swiss cross-bow bolt was claimed as belonging to William Tell, and so on.

On the whole, Princess Izabela insisted on signed and sealed attestations of authenticity, and she filed these away scrupulously. But wishful thinking sometimes got the better of her common sense, and she often gave credit to dubious attributions. Her husband poked fun at her on this score, once presenting her with an old bedroom slipper of his own with a note attesting that it was the shoe of Gengis Khan.

One of those she had to watch closely was her friend General Michał Sokolnicki. In 1810, after a severe illness, this old soldier spent a few months convalescing at Puławy under the care of Princess Izabela, and was enthralled by her project. He obtained prolonged leave from the army and went to take the waters in Germany, which he scoured on her behalf. His quest was favoured by circumstance, as many old buildings, particularly those in the gothic style so despised by the Enlightenment, were being allowed to crumble. He was able to remove many architectural details and 37 stained-glass windows from various ruined churches, including the chapel of Charlemagne at Aix-la-Chapelle. These reached Puławy, not without some damage, and most were fitted into the windows of the Gothic House (unfortunately no trace of them has survived the depredations of war). He also bought a corpus of magnificent illuminated manuscripts from the fifteenth century which are to this day the pride of the Czartoryski Library. Characteristically, these were described by him as 'Books and manuscripts whose text, notes or provenance relates to famous people or to great historical events'.

Soldiers feature prominently among the donors to the Gothic House, which was no coincidence. Those who fought alongside the French in places such as Italy and Spain were ideally placed to serve Izabela's purpose. It was an officer serving there who had the idea of plucking a sprig of myrtle from a bush in the Alhambra and sending it to Princess Izabela as a memento of the defeat of the Moors. From Avignon, another sent her relics of Petrarch and Laura, from Verona a third contributed a fragment from the alleged grave of Romeo and Juliet.

Another who sent her things from Italy was her son Adam Jerzy, who had found himself there as a result of a curious series of events. In 1795 he had been ordered to St Petersburg with his brother Konstanty as a hostage to the good behaviour of his parents. While at the Russian court, Prince Adam Jerzy grew close to the Grand Duke and future Tsar Alexander, and fell in love with his wife Elizaveta Alekseyevna. Alexander appears not to have minded, and the romance flourished, but his father Tsar Paul was less accommodating when news of the affair reached him. Prince Adam Jerzy was spared some of the more unpleasant forms of punishment meted out by the Russian court, and was instead sent off to Italy as the Russian ambassador to the king of Sardinia. It was a largely fictitious appointment, allowing the prince to spend time in Florence and then Rome, where he remained until 1801. He was in frequent correspondence with his mother, and kept her supplied with objects for the museum, mainly architectural elements. He even indulged in some amateur excavation work in the Forum Romanum, much of which was then still a heap of overgrown rubble.

In 1801 Prince Adam Jerzy presented his mother with something of a problem, when he sent her two pictures he had bought in Italy. One was a portrait of a young man by Raphael. She did not know what to do with it at first, because the sitter could not be identified. Finally, she decided that the artist himself had an important enough profile in the history of European art to warrant its inclusion as being associated with him – not, let it be noted, as an example of his art. The other picture was easier to accommodate. It was a portrait of a young lady holding an ermine, by Leonardo da Vinci. It was quickly decided that this was a portrait of the legendary 'Belle Ferronière' who had been the mistress of Francis I of France, and although he was already 'covered' by his hunting-flask, there was no harm in honouring the memory of this great monarch through a second object. Princess Izabela had the words 'La Belle Ferronière' painted across the front of the picture, and found a place on the wall for it.

Disaster

The quirky nature of the collections at Puławy and the way they were exhibited can all too easily obscure the true essence of Princess Izabela's project, which was serious and, in some ways, very modern. This apparently frivolous self-indulgence of a grand lady's hobby was from the beginning a public-spirited enterprise, and it was her intention to donate her museum to the nation, along with an endowment adequate for its upkeep.

The uneducated little girl who did not know what to say to Rousseau had come a long way. She had acquired knowledge and the self-assurance to spread her message, which was one of passionate inclusive patriotism. She founded free schools for village children and encouraged others to do likewise. In 1817 she wrote and published a simple history of Poland for children which was at the same time a catechism of civic virtue. She presided over various social initiatives, including a commission which defended womens' right to a minimum wage.

All this lent Princess Izabela an authority which explains how she managed to engage the wholehearted support of her children, of individuals such as Sokolnicki, Beydaels, Lenoir and Denon, of church authorities which allowed her to rummage through tombs, of the University of Kraków, of the Jagiellon Library, of various provincial educational institutions, of municipal authorities, and even of humble villagers. She managed to enthuse an increasingly wide circle of people from almost every social class in her project. And it was ultimately this that ensured the success of the enterprise. For the museum was about people – living people as well as dead ones.

It was also about politics. The lower chamber of the Temple was a sort of crypt dedicated to the armed struggle for independence during her own lifetime. It was dominated by a black marble obelisk to the memory of Prince Józef Poniatowski, the epitome of that struggle, who had met a heroic death at the battle of Leipzig in 1813. The walls were adorned with shields representing the Legions founded in Italy in 1797 by General Dąbrowski and the Polish Army of the Duchy of Warsaw. The relics and their arrangement gave it the appearance of a lodge in which Poland's resurrection was being plotted. The intrinsically political nature of the museum placed it in the front rank of the Polish struggle for survival – and by the same token condemned it to suffer all the vicissitudes of that struggle.

After its annihilation in 1795, the Polish state had been partially reincarnated as the

Prince Adam Jerzy Czartoryski, by N.I. Argunov, 1795

Duchy of Warsaw in 1807. The Congress of Vienna in 1815 essentially sanctioned the partitions, while moving some territory from Prussian domination to the Russian. The Russian share was renamed the Kingdom of Poland, but its king was in fact the Tsar of Russia. This 'Congress Kingdom', as it was often referred to, had a liberal constitution which permitted the Poles to carry on their cultural existence without hindrance. The Czartoryskis and their relatives held high office – Prince Adam Jerzy had actually drafted the constitution. But this marriage of a small liberal Polish state to a huge autocratic Russian empire was an unnatural one, and the strain began to tell in the 1820s. The Tsar trampled freedoms guaranteed by the Polish constitution. Young men remonstrated and conspired, and the Russian secret police went into action. The climate deteriorated with the accession in 1825 of Alexander's brutish brother Nicholas I.

Encouraged by the 1830 July Revolution in France and the Belgian rising in September of the same year, a group of young patriots staged a revolution in Warsaw on the night of 29 November 1830. They took to the streets and disarmed Russian troops stationed in the capital, but they had no plan beyond the slogan of national independence, and no leaders. In the ensuing political vacuum, Prince Adam Jerzy Czartoryski found himself acclaimed as the head of the nation in arms. He had always been opposed to armed struggle, believing that more could be achieved for his country by peaceful means, but he could not refuse the leadership. There followed ten months of unequal war, during which the Polish armies won several resounding victories but were eventually defeated.

On 6 December 1830, a week after the outbreak of the insurrection, Russian forces that had been obliged to evacuate Warsaw marched into Puławy. Despite her advanced age, Princess Izabela reacted with energy at the news of their approach. She closed the Temple of the Sibyl and the Gothic House and began packing up, hiding and evacuating the collection. She got some local units of the Polish army to save part of the archive before the Russians seized it. The salvage work carried on as the fighting intensified and the house at Puławy was bombarded by Russian artillery, ironically under the command of Princess Izabela's grandson, Prince Adam Ludwig of Württemberg. When the time came for her to leave, she took the the Royal Casket with her in the same carriage.

The defeat of the November Insurrection was a personal tragedy for Prince Adam

Jerzy. Proscribed and condemned to death, executed in effigy, he had to flee across Europe like a hunted criminal. It was also a financial disaster for him. Puławy and all his property within the Congress Kingdom was confiscated, leaving him with only a large but not very productive estate under Austrian rule, at Sieniawa.

Princess Izabela, now 85 years old, retired to Sieniawa, where she lived out the four years left to her. But Prince Adam could not just set up house quietly in some out-of-the-way spot, leading a frugal life until his finances recovered. He felt it his duty to carry on the struggle and do everything in his power to reverse the defeat of his country. He went to Paris, capital of the only Great Power sympathetic to Poland. He gathered a number of capable people together and opened offices in places as diverse as London and Istanbul to monitor the political situation, report on any event or circumstance that might be used to Poland's advantage, and to keep stating the Polish case forcefully.

He left the matter of sorting out the family finances and material establishment to his wife and his mother-in-law, the canny Princess Anna Sapieha. These ladies did extremely well. They quickly realised that the Paris of the 1830s, in the first exuberant flush of the 'bourgeois' July monarchy, held ample opportunities for enrichment, and the family's finances improved markedly. The Czartoryskis rented apartments and then an *hotel particulier* in central Paris, but by the beginning of the 1840s they felt the need for something permanent. It would have to be large enough to accommodate not only the whole family and its retinue, but also the Prince's secretariat. It would also have to lend itself to entertaining on a grand scale.

It was the painter Eugène Delacroix who, through the agency of his friend the composer Fryderyk Chopin, solved their problem. One day in 1843 he came across a derelict house on the Ile Saint Louis that was about to be pulled down. It was an *hotel particulier* built in 1642 for a senior treasury official by the name of Nicolas Lambert de Thorigny. Its creators were the architect Louis Le Vau in collaboration with the two painters Charles Le Brun and Eustache Le Sueur – a trio that was to prove so ideally matched that they were called upon to start work on the projected royal palace of Versailles a couple of years later. The building had last been inhabited during Napoleonic days, and was now scheduled for demolition, as the City of Paris wanted the land for a new public library. The Czartoryskis bid against the city at the auction and won.

The Hotel Lambert is a magnificent building, one of the greatest expressions of French *grand siècle* classicism, and the closest France ever came to the baroque. It is also very grand, with a layout which could accommodate any amount of pomp and ceremony. Apart from being a family house, it inevitably became a kind of court. The *Familia* had never missed an opportunity to stress their Jagiellon origins, and some of Prince Adam's supporters promoted the idea of him as king of a restored Poland. Foreigners generally like to simplify things, and a large section of French society simply regarded the Czartoryskis as the royal family of Poland.

Sheltering in the shadows of the Hotel Lambert were a number of emigré institutions; a Polish Young Ladies' Institute, a school for young men, a Polish Library, the Polish Literary and Historical Society, and even a newspaper. The Hotel Lambert itself was also the political headquarters of Prince Adam, housing his offices, archive, secretariat and so on. So it was, in effect, the seat of a government in exile – the very name of the building became, like the Quai d'Orsay or Downing Street, synonymous with a political unit.

It also became an important social and cultural landmark, and it is in this function that it fulfilled its most significant role. Practically all the principal Polish writers and artists had turned up in Paris after the debacle of 1831. Some, like the poet Zygmunt Krasiński and the composer Fryderyk Chopin, were close friends of the Czartoryski family from Warsaw days, but even for those who were not, it was natural to congregate at the Hotel Lambert. The Czartoryskis gave soirées and receptions for the Polish and French aristocracy, and these occasions were frequented by the poets and other artists – and not only Polish ones. Lamartine, George Sand, Balzac, Berlioz and Liszt were among those who frequented the princess' soirées.

By the mid-1840s the Hotel Lambert had become the greatest centre of Polish life – political, cultural and social – outside Poland, and it began to develop an iconic quality that carried far beyond this. It came to stand for Polishness itself, for political rectitude, morality, dedication to the cause and, perhaps most significantly, for national culture. Thus the Hotel Lambert had quite naturally taken on much of what Puławy had stood for since the 1780s.

Aigrette worn on a fur cap by King Stephen Bathory (1575–1586)

Teutonic knight's sword captured at the battle of Grunwald in 1410

Act of the Union of Horodło between Poland and Lithuania in 1413

Illumination by Barthélémy d'Eyck for the *Livre des Tournois* by René the Good of Anjou, 1465–1475

Illuminations showing the rituals of election of a king of Poland, from the Pontifical of Bishop Erazm Ciołek, by an unknown Kraków artist ca. 1510

Portrait of Queen Izabella of Denmark, by the Master of the Legend of St Mary Magdalene, Brussels ca.1500, thought by Princess Izabela to be that of Anne Boleyn

AVE GRACIA
PLENA DOMI
NVS TECVM

The Annunciation, by Dieric Bouts, Louvain, ca. 1470 (*above*)

The Annunciation, from a triptych by Master George, 1517, rescued from the Wawel by Princess Izabela (*opposite*)

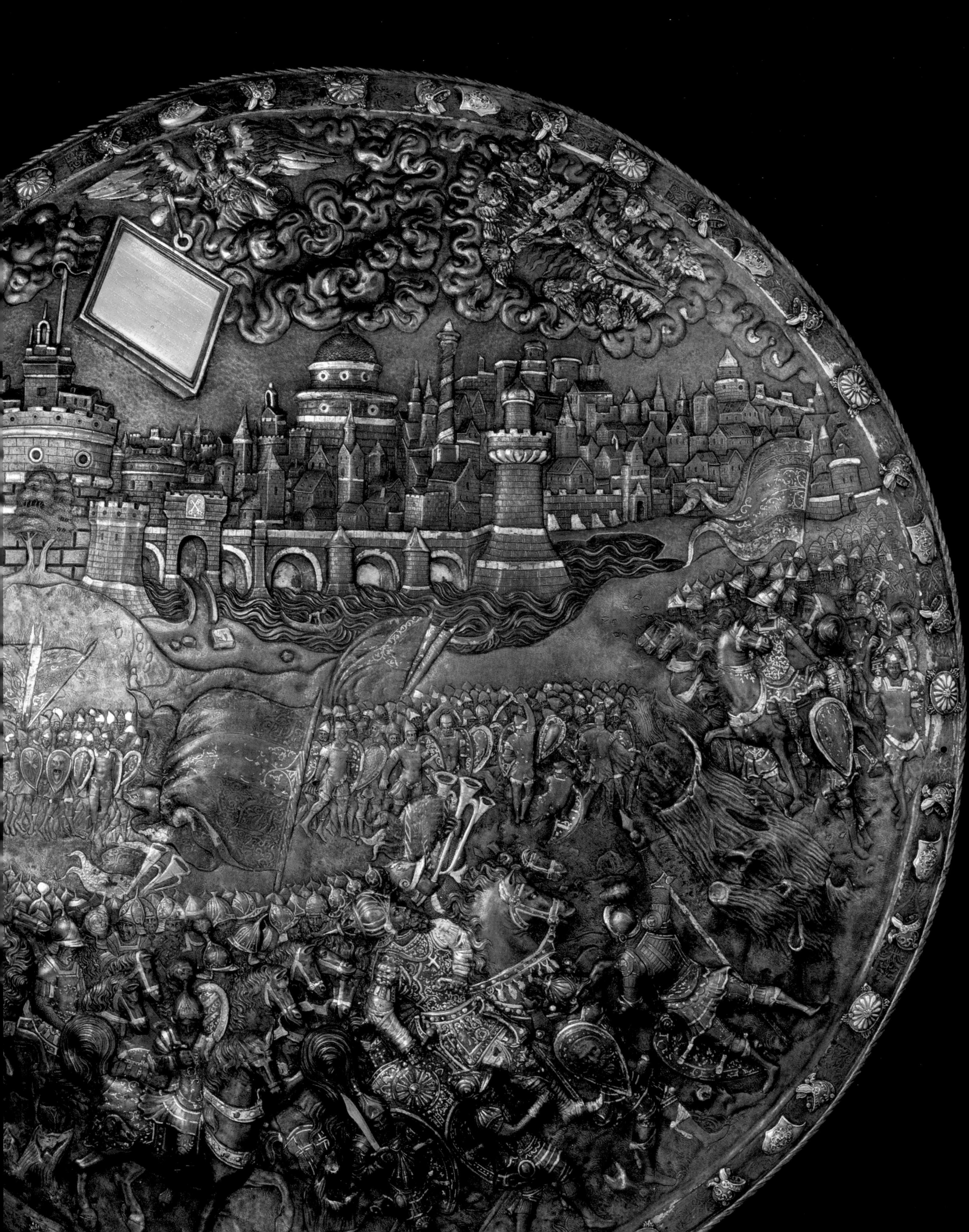

Venus Victrix, by Michele Tosini alias Ridolfo del Ghirlandaio (*above*)

The 'Augury shield', Italy, sixteenth century (*opposite*)

NICOLAI COPERNICI

net, in quo terram cum orbe lunari tanquam epicyclo contineri
diximus. Quinto loco Venus nono mense reducitur. Sextum
deniq; locum Mercurius tenet, octuaginta dierum spacio circū
currens. In medio uero omnium residet Sol. Quis enim in hoc

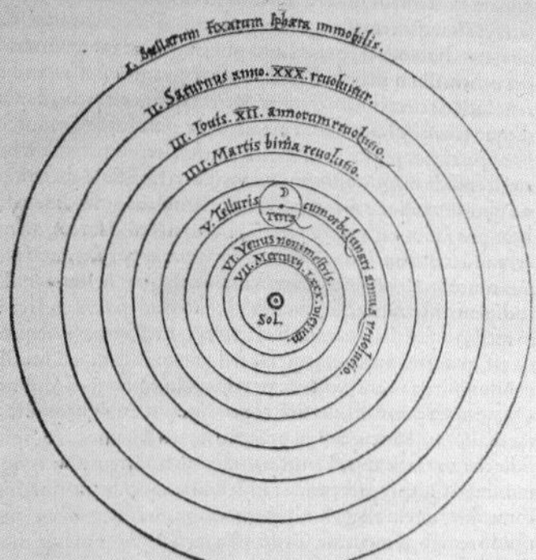

pulcherrimo templo lampadem hanc in alio uel meliori loco po
neret, quàm unde totum simul possit illuminare? Siquidem non
inepte quidam lucernam mundi, alij mentem, alij rectorem uo-
cant. Trimegistus uisibilem Deum, Sophoclis Electra intuentē
omnia. Ita profecto tanquam in solio regali Sol residens circum
agentem gubernat Astrorum familiam. Tellus quoq; minime
fraudatur lunari ministerio, sed ut Aristoteles de animalibus
ait, maximā Luna cū terra cognationē habet. Concipit interea à
Sole terra, & impregnatur annuo partu. Inuenimus igitur sub
hac

REVOLVTIONVM LIB. I. 10

hac ordinatione admirandam mundi symmetriam, ac certū har
moniæ nexum motus & magnitudinis orbium: qualis alio mo-
do reperiri non potest. Hic enim licet animaduertere, nō segni-
ter contemplanti, cur maior in Ioue progressus & regressus ap-
pareat, quàm in Saturno, & minor quàm in Marte: ac rursus ma
ior in Venere quàm in Mercurio. Quodq; frequentior appare-
at in Saturno talis reciprocatio, quàm in Ioue: rarior adhuc in
Marte, & in Venere, quàm in Mercurio. Præterea quòd Satur
nus, Iupiter, & Mars acronycti propinquiores sint terræ, quàm
circa eorū occultationem & apparitionem. Maxime uero Mars
pernox factus magnitudine Iouem æquare uidetur, colore dun-
taxat rutilo discretus: illic autem uix inter secundæ magnitudinis stellas inuenitur, sedula obseruatione sectantibus cognitus.
Quæ omnia ex eadem causa procedunt, quæ in telluris est motu. Quòd autem nihil eorum apparet in fixis, immensam illorū
arguit celsitudinem, quæ faciat etiam annui motus orbem siue
eius imaginem ab oculis euanescere. Quoniā omne uisibile lon
gitudinem distantiæ habet aliquam, ultra quam non amplius
spectatur, ut demonstratur in Opticis. Quòd enim à supremo
errantium Saturno ad fixarum sphæram adhuc plurimum in-
tersit, scintillantia illorum lumina demōstrant. Quo indicio ma
xime discernuntur à planetis, quodq; inter mota & non mota,
maximam oportebat esse differentiam. Tanta nimirum est diui
na hæc Opt. Max. fabrica.

De triplici motu telluris demonstratio. Cap. XI.

CVm igitur mobilitati terrenę tot tantaq; errantium
syderum consentiant testimonia, iam ipsum motum
in summa exponemus, quatenus apparentia per ipsum tanquā hypotesim demonstrentur, quē triplicē
omnino oportet admittere. Primum quem diximus νυχθημέρινον
à Græcis uocari, diei noctisq; circuitum proprium, circa axem
telluris, ab occasu in ortum uergentem, prout in diuersum mun
dus ferri putatur, æquinoctialem circulum describendo, quem
nonnulli æquidialem dicunt, imitantes significationem Græco
c ij rum,

Enamel portrait of a man by Leonard Limosin, 1546 (*above*)

King Zygmunt II Augustus' copy of Nicolaus Copernicus' *De Revolutionibus Orbium Coelestium*, 1543 (*opposite*)

Set of miniatures from the workshop of Lucas Cranach the Younger, ca. 1556, depicting, from top left: King Zygmunt I the Old, his wife Bona Sforza, King Zygmunt II Augustus, his first wife Elizabeth of Austria, his second wife Barbara Radziwi¢ ¢; bottom left: his third wife Catherine of Austria, his sisters Katarzyna, Zofia and Anna

Part of a suit of armour for rider and horse made in Milan ca. 1598 for Archduke Albrecht VII of the Netherlands

Hungarian-style *Buława* or baton of command of Hetman Jan Zamoyski, last quarter of the sixteenth century

The banner of Tsar Vasilii IV Shuyski, captured at the battle of Kłuszyn in 1610

SVPREMVS REGNI MARSCHA.
LEZAYSC. KOSCIERZEN: SREMEN
WALECEN: KOLEN ODOLANOV:
KAMIONA. LOSICEN RVBIESZOW
VISCEN: PILEN: GIERANOW:
SIFMIEN: METELEN: WOLBRAM
PREFECTVS

ortrait of Łukasz Opaliński as Marshal of oland, by an unknown Polish artist, ca. 1640

taff of office of the Marshal of ne Polish parliament (the Sejm), econd half of the seventeenth century

Silver-mounted conch in the form of a peacock, by Georg Hoffmann of Breslau, ca. 1600

Portrait of a lady by Gonzalez Cocques, acquired by Princess Izabela in the belief that it was a portrait of the Countess of Pembroke by Van Dyck

LADY PEMBROCK

Landscape with the Good Samaritan, by Rembrandt Harmensz. van Rijn, 1638

Portrait of a boy in Polish costume, by Caspar Netscher, The Hague, second half of the seventeenth century

Polish winged hussar armour, reconstructed with late seventeenth-century and early eighteenth-century elements (*opposite*)

A suit of Polish fish-scale armour belonging to Hetman Mikołaj Sieniawski, early eighteenth century (*below*)

Turkish shield and stirrups, captured by Hetman Mikołaj Sieniawski at the relief of Vienna in 1683

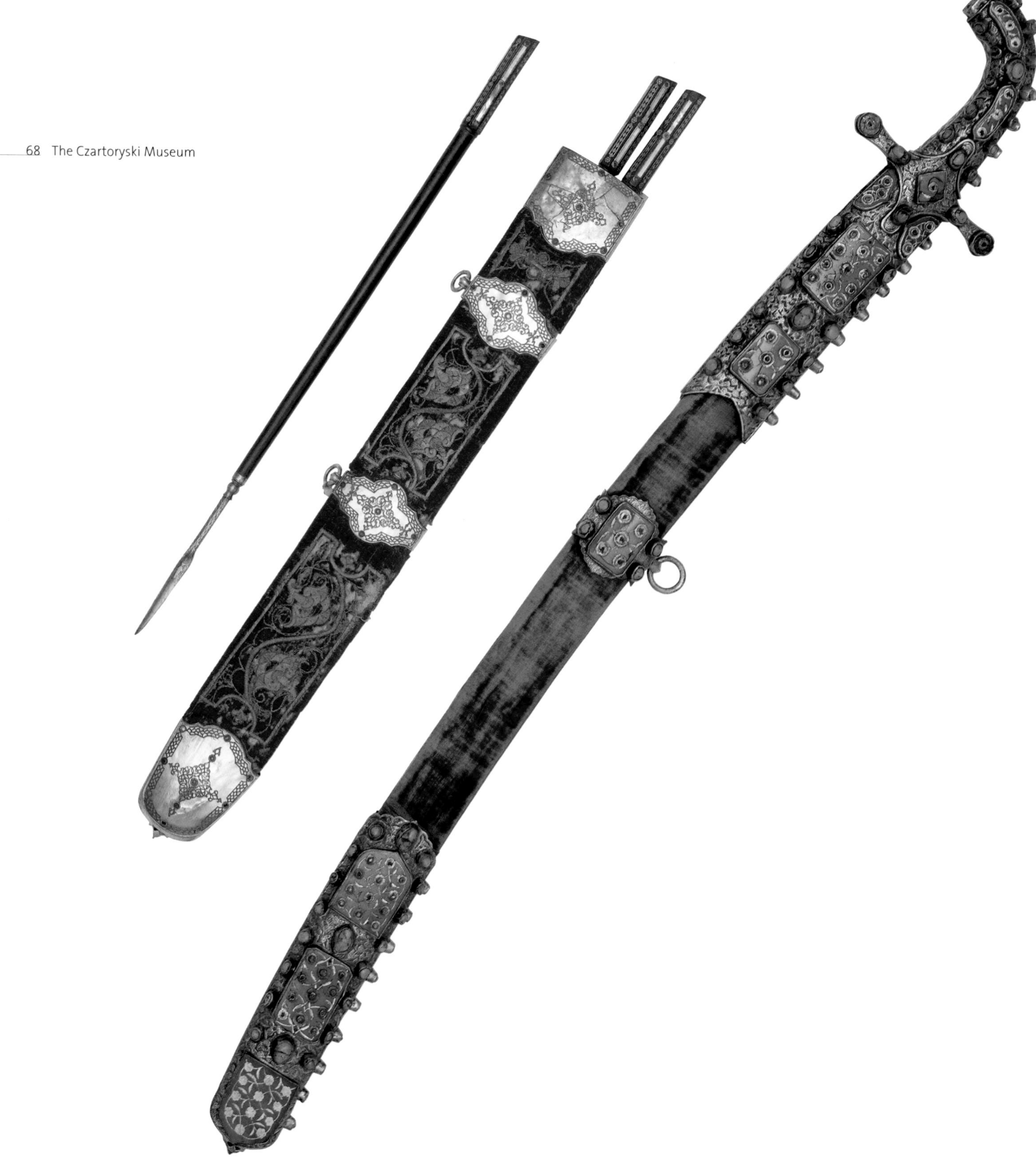

Turkish arrow-quiver, sabre and saddle, captured by Hetman Mikołaj Sieniawski at the relief of Vienna in 1683

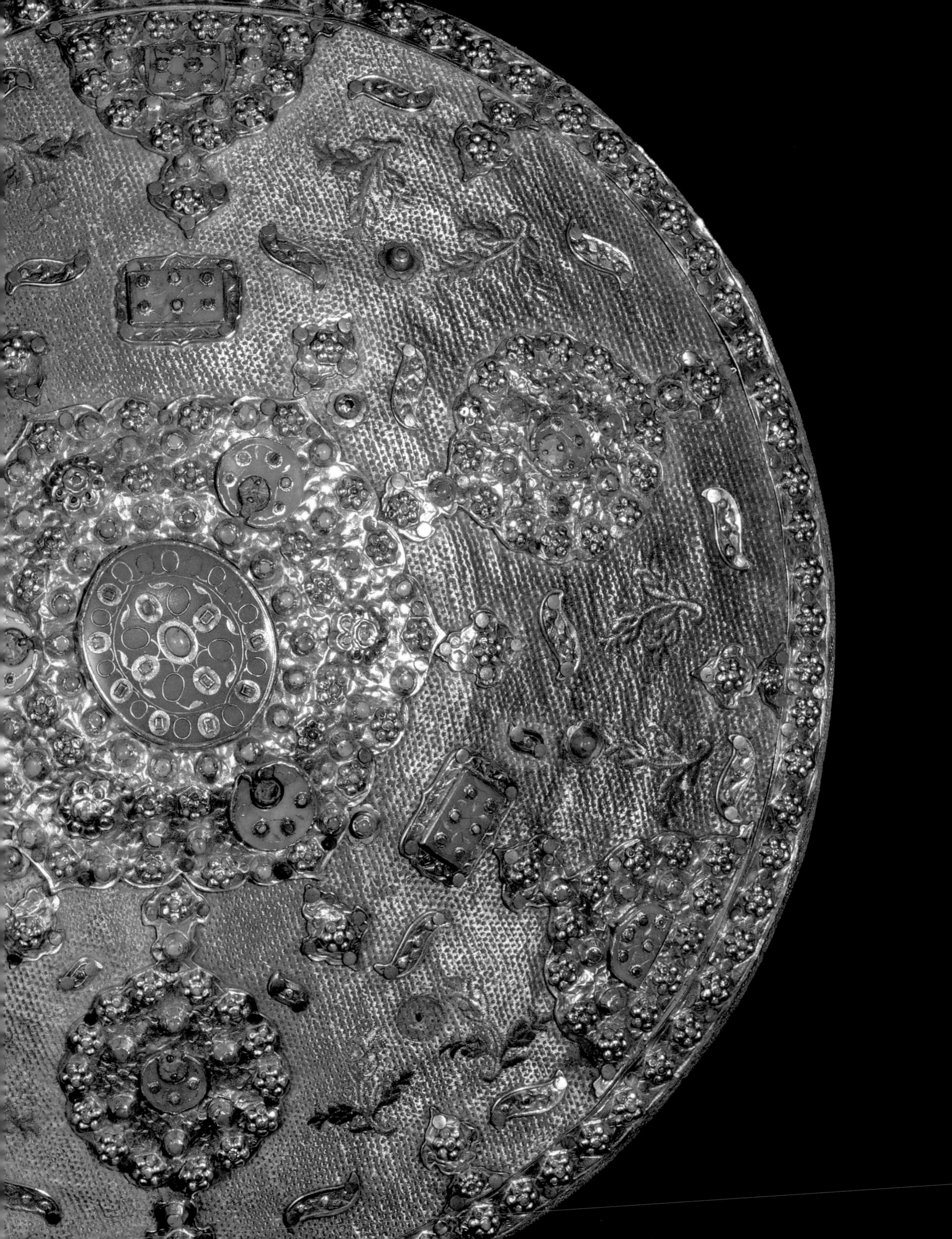

ırkish shield captured by Hetman Mikołaj Sieniawski at the
lief of Vienna in 1683, and his *Buława* or baton of command

Banquet given by the Grand Vizier in honour of Jan Trach Gniński, Polish ambassador to the Sublime Porte in 1677, by Pierre Paul Sevin, 1679

Scene from a Polish seventeenth-century banquet, showing the young St Stanisław Kostka fainting at the sound of bad language, by Georg Henner, 1774

Ming dynasty bowl with saucer, decorated with precious stones in Turkey in the seventeenth century

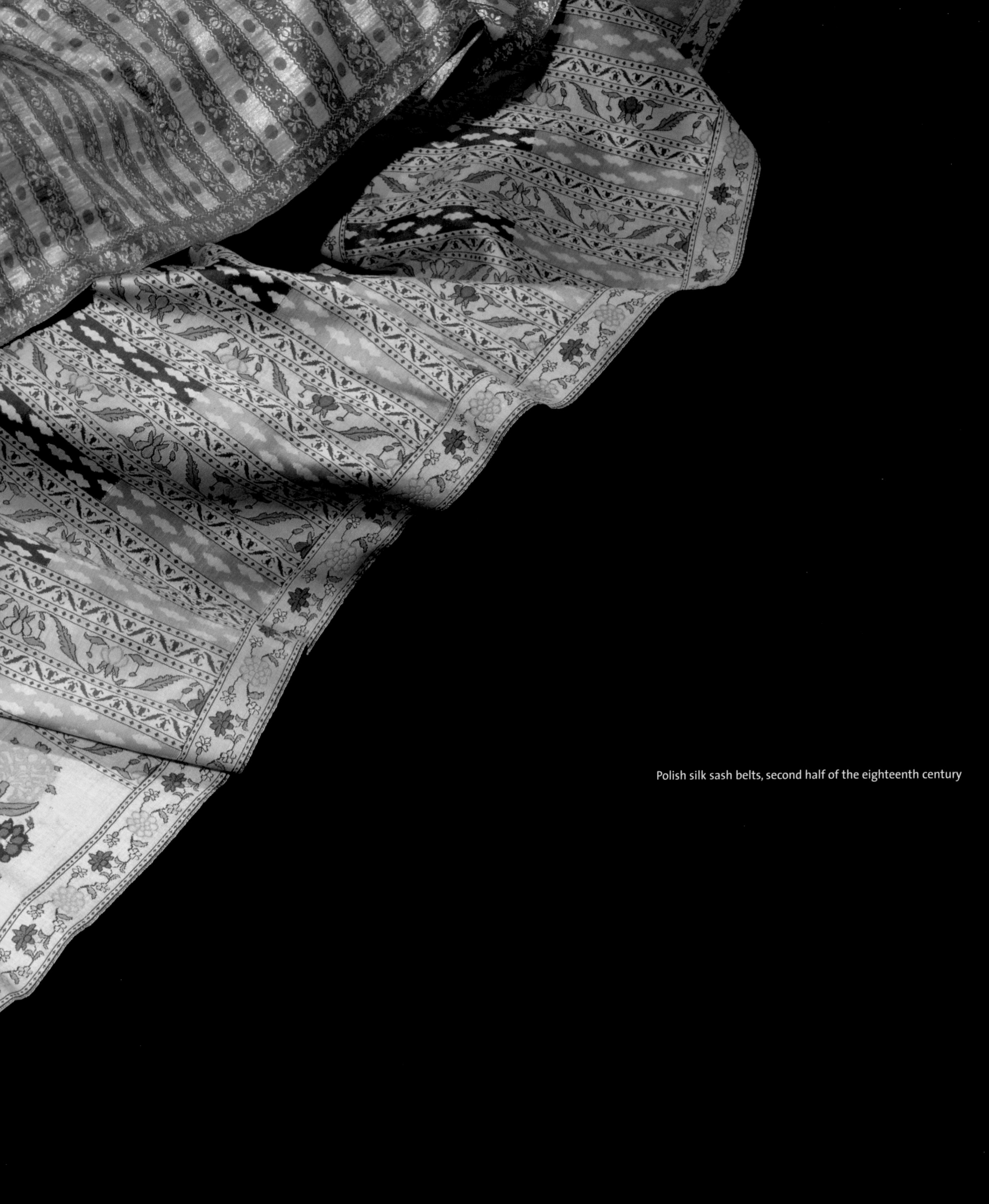

Polish silk sash belts, second half of the eighteenth century

VIVAT

Muscovite *kovsh* with the imperial arms, Moscow, 1701,
brought back from the 1812 campaign by a Polish soldier
Silver and gilt jug, by Ignacy Mietelski of Warsaw, ca. 1720
Silver and gilt tankard by Christian Pichgiel of Gdańsk, 1681–1700
(*above*)

Silver-gilt nef by Ezaias zu Linden of Nuremberg,
first quarter of the seventeenth century (*opposite*)

Lady with an Ermine, by Leonardo da Vinci,
probably the portrait of Cecilia Gallerani, painted ca. 1490

A New Mission

A Princely Collection

One of the aims of Hotel Lambert policy was to convince public opinion in the outside world that Poland was a worthy object of interest and support. This was no easy task, as few people in a place like Paris had any precise idea of where Poland lay or what it represented. The manner in which the Czartoryskis lived and the image of Poland projected by their court, rich as it was in cultural and artistic figures, was not enough. Poland's past needed to be put on display, her former splendour strongly underlined. In this context, the remnants of the Puławy collection suddenly assumed a new importance and found a new role to play.

The majority of the objects that had graced the Temple of the Sibyl and the Gothic House had, miraculously, survived, but they were scattered all over Poland, often stored in very poor conditions, and the whereabouts of some were unknown. When Princess Izabela began her salvage operation at Puławy in December 1830, she took advantage of any opportunity, and sent things off for safekeeping in a number of different directions, often in haste, under cover of night. The library was stored partly in a local monastery and partly in Warsaw, but odd volumes of autograph manuscripts, incunabula and prints were also given to individuals for safekeeping. Some inevitably went astray in the successive moves.

Batches of objects were sent off to the houses of friends or family. The Zamoyskis at nearby Kozłówka and Podzamcze were an obvious choice. But much safer was the Zamoyski house at more distant Klemensów in Galicia, where most of the arms were duly transported and hidden. An important consignment was delivered to the Sapiehas at Krasiczyn, also in Galicia, where the most precious paintings, including the Leonardo, the Raphael and the Rembrandt, were walled up in the cellars. No proper list was made of what had been taken where – only the most valuable and important objects could be monitored in the confused wartime evacuation of Puławy. The process had involved dozens of local people, including simple servants, gardeners, peasants, priests, at least one village doctor and a family of Jewish traders. The need to keep the objects' movements secret reduced talk and correspondence to a minimum. Many other problems filled people's minds in these difficult times, and in some cases those with whom objects had been left preferred to forget entirely about their existence.

The Russian authorities feared the collections for the very reason for which Princess

Izabela had conceived the idea of creating them – they were a testimony to Poland's national past. The Russian police therefore tracked their movements as they might pursue dangerous subversives, and any person found in possession could expect to meet with unpleasant consequences. The eternal fear of paper that animates all despotic regimes, particularly Russian ones, meant that it was the library and the archive which were in greatest danger. In 1830 the Russians had seized 47 crates of books and 1,816 engravings at Puławy. But the rest had been spirited away. Most had only been moved to secret locations within the Kingdom of Poland, and as soon as the dust settled after 1831 they were removed to Sieniawa and Kraków beyond the reach of Russia. This involved dangerous nocturnal expeditions across a border patrolled by cossacks.

The Austrian authorities were not, like the Russians, determined to extirpate Polish culture. But the Austria of the 1830s and 1840s was the Austria of Metternich, and her

The house at Sieniawa, by Juliusz Kossak, 1873

Prince Władysław Czartoryski

authorities were certainly not willing to abet the Czartoryski family in flouting regulations imposed by her Russian ally. The collection and the books brought to Sieniawa and elsewhere in Austrian-ruled Poland therefore had to be kept hidden. When the Austrians annexed the hitherto free city of Kraków, after the disturbances of 1848, that part of the archive and library stored there had to be evacuated to Paris. The most politically sensitive of the books stored at Sieniawa soon followed.

In 1852, on Prince Adam Sapieha's wedding-day, there was a fire at Krasiczyn which destroyed most of the castle. The Czartoryski treasures stored in the cellars escaped unharmed, but they could not be left in what would now be an uninhabited ruin. So they too were sent to Paris. People who had hidden smaller quantities or single objects brought them out of hiding and despatched them to Paris by whatever means they could. Larger consignments, such as those stored by Count Jan Zamoyski at Kozłówka, were similarly smuggled out, while the things taken in by Count Tytus Działyński at Kórnik left for Paris more overtly. But it was still a dangerous business. The Tsarist police kept a watchful eye, and there were some tragic losses – part of the archives had to be burnt because the police were on their trail, and in 1853 a number of historical mementoes from the Temple of the Sibyl hidden by a local parish priest were discovered and confiscated. The attitude of the Russian authorities softened after the empire's defeat in the Crimean War, making it less risky to handle such objects. And there were also some happy surprises; in 1869, during rebuilding works at Klemensów, Count Tomasz Zamoyski uncovered a large cache of arms and armour from the Temple of the Sibyl that had been walled up by his father for safekeeping in 1831 and subsequently forgotten about.

When they reached Paris, the objects were not at first treated as a museum collection, but worked into the interior furnishing and decor of the house. Neither Prince Adam Jerzy nor his wife had ever been as taken with the collections as his mother, and what he appreciated in them now was their 'political' value as a backdrop to his establishment. Adam Jerzy, born in 1770, was growing old, and from the mid-1850s he had gradually drawn his younger son, Władysław, into his political work. When he died in 1861, it was Władysław rather than the sickly elder son Witold who took over as head of the Hotel Lambert political machine.

Born in 1828, Prince Władysław had from an early age been groomed to become a worthy successor to his father. In 1855, he had been married to Maria Amparo Countess de Vista Allegre, daughter of queen Christina of Spain by her morganatic union with the Duke of Riancares, an economically and politically interesting match. Prince Władysław took on his father's mantle and carried it during the January Insurrection of 1863, mobilising the Hotel Lambert in support of the doomed uprising against Russia. But with the collapse of the insurrection in 1864 he could justifiably conclude that there was no useful purpose to be served by pursuing the struggle. He wound down the political machine of the Hotel Lambert, leaving in place only its propaganda and educational elements. His heart had never been in the role that had settled on his father and threatened to envelop him too.

The urge to collect, however, re-emerged in Prince Władysław and his sister Izabela. She too had been married off for political purposes and much against her will, to Count Jan Działyński, the foremost conservative patriot and magnate in Prussian-ruled Poland. But the couple quickly came to an arrangement to live apart, and she was left free to indulge her passion for collecting.

The Second Empire in France was a period when collections were built up (and dispersed) with unprecedented speed, and it was also a period when the whole subject of collecting and its methodology first attracted serious study. Thus the very existence of the Czartoryski collection became of interest. In 1865 a selection of 388 objects from the collection were shown in a 'Polish Room' at that year's *Exposition des Arts Décoratifs*, and they were much admired. Johann Strauss even composed a waltz entitled 'Les Trésors de la Pologne', the sheet music decorated with reproductions of objects from the collection. Elements of the collection were put on view

Countess Izabela Działyńska, née Czartoryska

again in 1878, at the *Grande Exposition Universelle*, where they filled a 'Polish Room'. It is perhaps worth noting here that it was as a result of these exhibitions that a certain type of silk-and-gold Persian carpet, well-represented in the Czartoryski as in other Polish collections but unknown elsewhere, was seen, admired, and assumed to be of Polish origin and therefore labelled '*tapis Polonais*' – an incongruous description that is still in general use.

This was the period when gallery-visiting became a favoured pastime of the leisured classes, and the Hotel Lambert opened its doors to the public, as we learn from a guide-book of Paris published in 1867. This places the Czartoryski collection '*en première ligne*' with half a dozen other private collections, but it does warn that these are not always easy to gain access to, before moving on to a general description of the collections. 'At the Hotel Lambert, for example, the principal wonders are armour, jewels and an infinite quantity of objets d'art,' it tells us, 'a portrait by Holbein of extraordinary beauty, a Clouet, a series of admirable little portraits by Cranach, an extremely rare landscape by Rembrandt, a few Italian portraits and many historical ones.'

Prince Władysław and his sister had similar tastes, which mirrored the taste of the time fairly closely. The sensations of the *wunderkammer*, the historical significance of works of art, the Romantic cult of association – all of which had lain at the core of the original collection – exerted no fascination on the mind of the 1850s. Prince Władysław's collecting was probably also governed in part by an unconscious reaction to his grandmother's legacy. While he remained faithful to the patriotic call and never let go an opportunity to purchase a good Polish object, he wanted to give the collection more universal significance, a serious edge and academic credibility. This meant expanding his holdings of earlier art. A *sine qua non* of intellectual and cultural credibility at this time was the whole area of antiquities. Hence the enrichment of the collection in the direction of Mesopotamia and Egypt, the acquisition of Greek, Etruscan and Roman objects. The taste of the times is also responsible for the strong accent on the applied arts which manifests itself in the Limoges enamels, the medieval ivory objects, the early glass, Italian majolica and Hispano-mauresque earthenware, the objects of vertu, the oriental miniatures and the illuminated manuscripts. Prince

Władysław and his sister went to all the great sales of the day and used the most prestigious dealers. They bought well, and most of their acquisitions were of a high standard. Some, like the collection of Limoges enamels, the Etruscan and Greek vases and the early glass, were outstanding.

Prince Władysław had for years been thinking of setting up the collection in such a way that it could fulfil the purpose for which it had been created, and this in effect meant moving it back on to Polish soil. In the late 1860s this began to seem possible. The Russian regime was still carrying on a repressive policy and was utterly unconducive to the Prince's intentions. The Prussian regime was also waging war on Polish culture, but it was possible, as Prince Władysław's sister Izabela had discovered on her estate of Gołuchów, to carry on cultural activity in a limited way in Prussian-ruled Poland. But it was the regime in the Austrian partition that had changed most radically. Shaken by revolt and defeat, the Habsburg monarchy had granted far-reaching autonomy to its regions, and its Polish subjects could now pursue their own cultural aspirations openly.

While Prince Władysław was considering his options, the collection was once again caught up in dramatic and dangerous events. With the French defeat in the Franco-Prussian war of 1870, Paris was threatened. The family had moved to London, taking with them a few of the most precious pieces, but the main corpus of the collection remained at the Hotel Lambert, where everything that was most valuable was taken down to the cellars. During the street-fighting between the troops of the Paris Commune and the French army in 1871, the Hotel Lambert was used as a Communard stronghold. It was attacked several times and took some direct hits. The only damage sustained was to the building and some of the furniture, but when Prince Władysław returned, he decided that enough was enough.

In 1874 the Council of the City of Kraków offered him a building, the old Arsenal, in which to house his collection if he wished to bring it back to Poland. He accepted, and in

Mummy case of Asetemachbit, priestess of the God Amon, Egypt, end of the tenth century BC

Athenian stamnos, by the 'Chicago painter', second half of the fifth century BC (*opposite*)

1776 the whole library was reunited under one roof, leaving only the political papers of the Hotel Lambert in Paris.

The objects presented greater problems. Prince Władysław and his sister Izabela had always collected together, as a team, but since she was intending to move back to Poland too, she wanted to take along some of the things they had bought to her castle of Gołuchów. In the event, she took the collection of Greek vases, some Etruscan antiquities, a small but exquisite collection of medieval applied arts, including enamels, glass, gold and ivory. She took none of the original Puławy pieces.

It was these that rightly belonged in any museum Prince Władysław might open in Kraków, and he was keen to put them on show there. But many of the Puławy pieces, including the Leonardo and most of the pictures, could legitimately be seen as part of the furnishings of the Prince's residence. And while he meant to spend more time in Poland and carried out major works at Sieniawa so that the house could receive the family in some comfort, neither he nor his French second wife, Princess Marguerite d'Orléans, grand-daughter of King Louis Philippe, could realistically contemplate burying themselves in the Galician countryside. Nor could there be any question of getting rid of the Hotel Lambert; it had become an institution in Paris and a landmark for the extended family. And, Polish history being what it was, there was no telling when it might come in useful again. Inevitably, therefore, the move back to Poland was a piecemeal affair, and it begged many questions about the shape the museum would assume in its new home of Kraków.

The Museum

The return of the Czartoryski collection to Poland in the 1870s could not take the shape of a return to the original form of the museum. Princess Izabela's idea had been very much of its time, and it had had its day, as had the idea of armed struggle for Polish independence. Times had changed, and Prince Władysław saw the mission of his family differently. This could no longer be an overtly political mission; the accent in Poland had changed to methodical organic work to improve and enlighten the nation. In the collection, Prince Władysław possessed not only a valuable national asset which he was bound to preserve and make accessible, but also a fount of education. He therefore proposed to refound the museum on more academic lines and to turn it into into a modern institution of learning.

In 1876 he purchased the building adjoining the Arsenal, a former monastic school of the Piarist Order, known as the *Klasztorek*, the 'little monastery'. In 1886 he acquired the house on the corner of Pijarska and Św Jana Streets, just across the street from the *Klasztorek*, and soon after that the adjacent premises on Św Jana Street. Together, they made up an extensive block, but all the properties were in a state of advanced dereliction, and had nothing in common except for their proximity. As well as repairing the structure and linking up the interiors to suit their new role, Prince Władysław also wanted to give the assemblage of buildings an appropriate exterior. For this, he looked to the founder of historicism in French architecture, Emmanuel Viollet-le-Duc, but he was too taken up with commissions in France, and never made it to Kraków. Prince

Bronze clasp, Poland, sixth–fifth century BC

Władysław's next choice was Viollet-le-Duc's son-in-law, Maurice Ouradou, who was doing some work for Izabela Działyńska at Gołuchów.

In 1878 Ouradou produced a design for the *Klasztorek* which turned this crumbling baroque exterior into a curious eclectic gothic mixing French and Polish characteristics. It was linked by a passage over the street to the other buildings, which were given a new façade designed by Albert Bitner and Zygmunt Hendel in a style that followed Ouradou's, adding only some Renaissance elements to marry it to the other buildings in the street. The homogenized whole was commonly referred to as 'the Palace'. These works were not finished completely until 1901, but as early as 1878 Prince Władysław placed over the entrance the inscription which announced the intention behind his work and the profile it was to adopt: 'Museum of the Princes Czartoryski, founded at Puławy in 1801, established in Kraków 1876'.

In his determination to turn the Museum into an academic institution, Prince Władysław excluded a number of Puławy objects which he found too sentimental, either leaving them at the Hotel Lambert or donating them to the Polish Library in Paris. Some objects acquired by his grandmother he restored to their place of origin – the stirrup of Kara Mustafa removed from the crucifix in Wawel Cathedral was returned there. In 1871 he donated a quantity of objects which did not fit in with his idea of the new museum to the Polish museum at Rapperswil in Switzerland. Others he donated to the archaeological department of the Jagiellon University. At the same time, he did not cease adding to the holdings, scouring foreign and home markets for new acquisitions.

An institution such as the Czartoryski Museum could not be run as a private hobby, and its administration was entrusted to a board, nominated by the Prince. In 1884 he appointed Marian Sokołowski, founder of the first Polish chair of Art History at the Jagiellon University, curator of the Museum. Sokołowski reorganized the collection, dividing it up according to material and technique. Artistic delectation and historical reflection had no place in the new Museum, which was to be a workshop of analysis and research. Many of the exhibits underwent restoration, and new frames, shelving and cases were provided: carved neo-Renaissance furniture for the *Klasztorek*, simple black cabinets for the collection of antiquities. Prince Władysław was also very keen to see the

collection properly catalogued, and Professor Sokołowski made a start on this process, which was to continue over the next decades, with catalogues of the various departments alternating with the publication of studies of some of the key pieces.

If the Museum was to flourish as an academic institution, it must, Prince Władysław realized, have a firm economic base. As far back as 1817 Prince Adam Jerzy had contemplated turning his estate into an inalienable entity limiting the rights of the owner and obliging him to preserve the collections. Prince Władysław followed this up and decided to establish an *ordynacja*, which entailed the whole estate and turned the owner into something closer to the incumbent of a throne than a full owner. One obstacle was the lack of interest displayed by his son August, the fruit of Prince Władysław's first marriage, to Princess Maria Amparo. He was a delicate boy with a strong religious sense. In 1887, to his father's chagrin, he became a priest and joined the Salesian Order, abdicating all responsibility for family affairs. He died of consumption six years later, bathed in the odour of sanctity. Princess Maria Amparo had died young, and Prince Władysław had re-married, this time Princess Marguerite d'Orléans. This union produced two sons, Adam Ludwik and Witold, and it was around the elder of these two that Prince Władysław now built his plans.

On 17 January 1897 the Emperor Francis Joseph signed the act setting up the Sieniawa *ordynacja*, with a principal consisting of land and buildings, movable property and capital assets estimated at 4.5 million Austrian crowns, which did not include the greatest asset of all, the collections. The decree contained clauses obliging the incumbent of the *ordynacja* to set aside certain sums for the upkeep of the collections, and others for the granting of scholarships.

Prince Adam Ludwik Czartoryski, first incumbent or *ordynat* of Sieniawa, was a model citizen, serving on various public bodies. In

Prince Adam Ludwik Czartoryski

1911 his younger brother Witold died, leaving him the Hotel Lambert and Gołuchów, which had also been turned into an *ordynacja* by Izabela Działyńska and left to him on her death. Prince Adam Ludwik cared for the two museums conscientiously, and although he did not share his forebears' passion for collecting, he did enrich the collections by a further 37 items, mainly Greek vases, and brought some objects back from his travels in Japan. It was his eighteen-year old wife Maria Ludwika Krasińska who took over the direction of things shortly after their marriage in 1902. She was a diminutive girl ten years his junior, but she was endowed with tremendous determination, and she had the self-assurance born of the fact that she was a great heiress in her own right.

The Czartoryski Museum had become established as a major cultural landmark on the Polish scene, and continued to play an increasingly important didactic role. But at this seemingly propitious juncture, the whole enterprise was once again threatened by the politics that had dogged it from the start. In 1914 war broke out, and Poland lay in the front line of hostilities between Russia and the Central Powers of Germany and Austria. In the event of the Russians entering Austrian Kraków, they could perfectly well help themselves to all those objects that had been at Puławy in 1830, since these were still subject to the confiscation decree. Prince Adam Ludwik had been called up to the Austrian army, and res- ponsibility for the Museum fell on the shoulders of Princess Maria Ludwika. Despite having five children and various other things to worry about, she reacted with decisiveness and speed.

Looking around for a safe haven for the most valuable pieces of the collection, she focused on Dresden. Thanks to the royal connections of the Czartoryskis, she had no difficulty in presenting her case, through members of the Saxon royal family, to the direction of the Royal Collections and asking that space be found in the *Gemäldegalerie* for a selection of the most valuable objects. These included 52 paintings, 12 carpets, 35 folders of prints and drawings, as well as the Rembrandt, the Raphael and the Leonardo. Although the objects were only open to viewing by the public on two days a week, they did arouse great interest and were seen by large numbers of Dresdeners.

But the interest aroused had unforeseen consequences. In the last days of the war, on 5 November 1918, Dr Hans Posse of the direction of the Royal Collections wrote to the

Princess Maria Ludwika Czartoryska, née Krasińska

Saxon ministry of internal affairs warning that the Czartoryskis would soon be thinking of removing their loan, and that such a valuable collection should under no circumstances be relinquished. With the collapse of German military might on the eastern front, Poland was in a state of unrest, and it looked as though it might slide towards Bolshevism, in the wake of Russia. But a few days later Józef Piłsudski took power in Warsaw, and on the same day the Saxon monarchy was toppled in Dresden. While Germany slid into instability, Poland proudly resumed her national independence.

In the event, it was not until 16 July 1920 that Princess Maria Ludwika signed the receipt confirming her recovery of all the objects. A couple of days later they returned to Kraków in what was now an independent Poland. And while the long-term outlook was by no means rosy, there were a number of new developments which promised much. The Bolshevik revolution in Russia had begun by revoking all decrees issued by the Tsars against other nations, and *inter alia*, it annulled the act of confiscation over the Czartoryskis' property. The 1921 Treaty of Riga between Russia and Poland provided for the return of all looted and confiscated works of art. The result was the return, in 1931, of a large number of books, archives and some objects taken from Puławy in 1831. Unfortunately, they did not return to the Czartoryski Museum but were placed in various national repositories.

The Museum's prestige grew under the new curator, Stefan Saturnin Komornicki, an art historian who wrote the first proper book about the Museum in 1929 and a pocket guide in 1938. This reflects the fact that it was by then attracting 12,000 visitors a year. The Museum and Library together employed seven curatorial staff and six servants. The rising cost of its upkeep impelled the Prince to approach the Polish government with a request for tax exemption. This proved fruitless, and Prince Adam Ludwik faced the future with a degree of anxiety. Repeated requests from abroad to buy some of the more famous paintings in the collection were nevertheless rejected out of hand. Prince Adam Ludwik died in 1937, and was succeeded by his son Prince Augustyn Józef, born in 1907. Augustyn was married to Princess Dolores Victoria Maria de los Mercedes Carlota de Borbon-Orléans, daughter of the Infante Don Carlos de Borbon y Borbon, Prince of the Asturias and heir to the throne of Spain during the minority of the future Alfonso XIII. Prince Augustyn and Princess Dolores were to play a vital role in the preservation of the collection.

iptych with Madonna and Child, by the Master of the Clares, Siena, st quarter of the thirteenth century (*opposite*)

ater Dolorosa, by Aelbrecht Bouts, beginning of the sixteenth century (*opposite*)

Anthony and St Lucy, from the workshop of Carlo Crivelli, ca. 1470 (*below*)

I·N·R·I

he martyrdom of St Sebastian, by a follower of the Master of Sigmaringen, Germany, eginning of the sixteenth century (*above*)

he Crucifixion, by the Master of the Pietà, Siena, 1350–1380 (*opposite*)

Cover of the Pułtusk Codex, Limoges, first half of the twelfth century

Enamelled processional crucifix, Limoges, 1225–1250

Book cover, Limoges, ca. 1150

The genealogy of Christ, from the Pułtusk Codex, Bavaria, ca. 1076

Ivory Virgin and Child, France, 1325–1350
(the crown was added in the nineteenth century) (*left*)

Reliquary casket, Limoges, ca. 1250 (*opposite*)

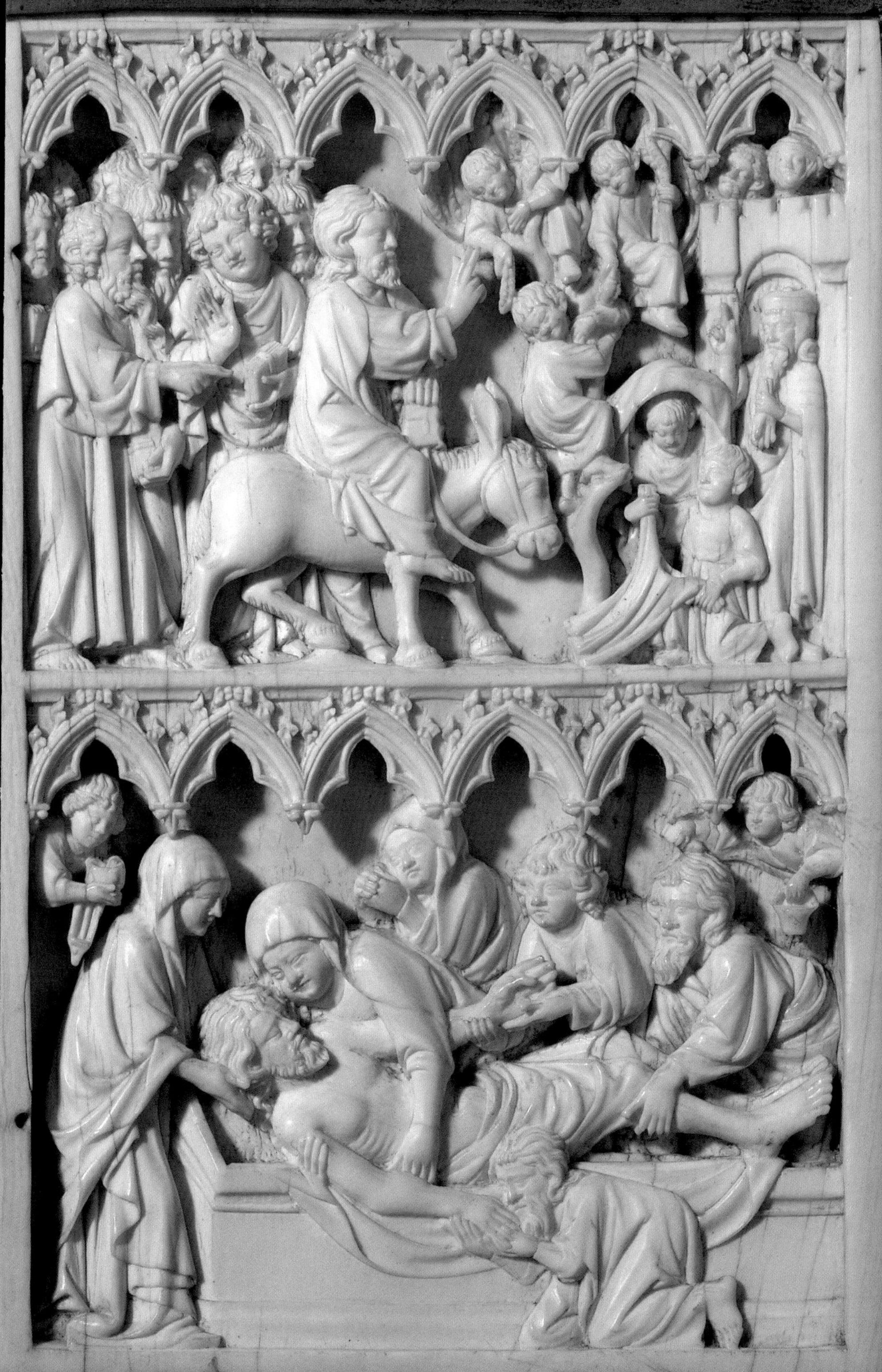

Silk, silver and gold embroidery from Flanders, ca. 1420, with scenes from the passion of Christ, originally for a liturgical cope, later made into an *antepedium* or altar-front for one of the chapels at Kraków's Wawel cathedral

Panel from a Florentine cassone, with scenes from the life of Lucretia, beginning of the fifteenth century

Florentine majolica dish, ca. 1460–70, depicting a mounted falconer

Majolica dish by 'the Master of the caricatures', Faenza, 1520–1525

The Good Samaritan, from *Traité de la Charité Chrétienne* by Nicolas Houel, ca. 1580

The Adoration of the Magi, by a follower of Stefan Lochner of Cologne, after 1450

The Annunciation, from the *Book of Hours* of Agnes de Kiquemberg by a follower of the Master of the Maréchal de Boucicault Paris, after 1420

St George and the dragon, from a Flemish prayerbook, by the Master of the Golden stems, 1420–1430

SCOPVS VITÆ CHRISTVS.
DE NOSTRE VRAY SALVT IESVS CHRIST EST LE BVT

vnigeniti a patre. Ple
ni gracie et veritatis.
In die Ephie. Secundu.
Mathe
natus esset ie
sus in bethle
em iude in dieby herodis

Omine labia mea
aperies.
Et os meum an
nunciabit laudem tuam.
Agnes de Kiquemberg dit Loen. en Genouix.

Three female heads, by Gerard David of Bruges, fifteenth–sixteenth century

Virgin and Child, by Vincenzo di Bagio Catena, 1495–1531

Brussels tapestry, ca. 1515–1520, depicting Danae being visited by Zeus in the form of a shower of gold (*above*)

Brussels tapestry, first quarter of the sixteenth century, representing the Virgin and Child with St Anne (*opposite*)

Amber chalice mounted in silver gilt, Koenigsberg, second half of the sixteenth century (*below*)

Amber tankard mounted in silver gilt, from the circle of Georg Schreiber and Andreas Meyer in Koenigsberg, ca. 1610 (*below*)

Amber and ivory devotional altar with scenes from the passion of Christ, by Michał Redlin, Gdańsk, second half of the seventeenth century (*opposite*)

Glass mosque lamp, Egypt or Syria, late fourteenth century

'Polonaise' rug, Persia, second half of the seventeenth century

ragment of an early seventeenth-century Persian silver-threaded
elvet hanging with a motif of young women watering chicory plants

ersian miniature depicting a gunmaker, by a painter working for
hah Abbas I, Isfahan, early seventeenth century

Sasanian silver cup, Persia, fifth–sixth century, excavated in eastern Poland at the beginning of the nineteenth century

Roman glass bowls, first half of first century

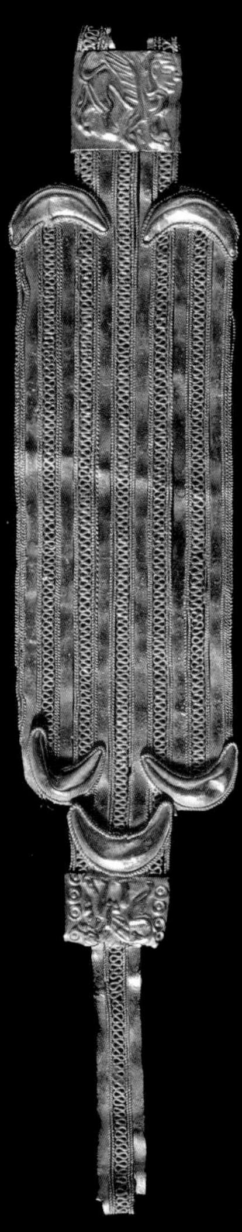

Etruscan braclets, eighth–seventh century BC

Marble head of a young woman from a funerary stela, Attica, ca. 350 BC

x, by the painter Onezimos, Athens, 500–480 BC

ck-figured krater, Athens, last quarter of the sixth century BC

Funerary stela of Merer, ruler of Upper Egypt, 2155–2040 BC

Terracota figure of Nike from Myrina in Asia Minor, first quarter of the second century BC

Struggle for Survival

War

As war loomed in the spring of 1939, Prince Augustyn faced an agonizing dilemma. All the talk was of the mass bombing expected to accompany modern warfare, and of the necessity of hiding people and things underground. The Museum prepared for war with sandbags and water-barrels. First-aid kits, gas-masks, buckets and spades were issued to every member of staff. But the Prince feared that Kraków would be captured early on in the course of the war, so he decided to safeguard the most precious elements of the collection by moving them to Sieniawa, which was further away from the German frontier. Sixteen cases were packed with antique gold objects, gems, illuminated manuscripts, carpets, arms and armour, prints, tapestries, the Royal Casket and 31 paintings. The Leonardo, the Rembrandt and the Raphael were packed separately. On 24 and 25 August the cases were transported to Sieniawa and stacked in a specially prepared shelter in the cellars of one of the outbuildings, which was then walled up.

On 1 and 2 September, as bombs rained down on Kraków, the last of the exhibits were carried down to the cellars. Prince Augustyn was at Sieniawa. He was not well, already suffering from the lung condition that would claim his life, and his wife was pregnant with their first son. When he received news that the Polish armies had been routed and were falling back, they set off in search of an alternative place of refuge for themselves and the sixteen cases, leaving the housekeeper in charge.

On 15 September German troops reached Sieniawa and took up quarters in the Czartoryski residence. Three days later, the housekeeper ventured into the outbuilding where the cases had been walled up, and found that the wall had been knocked through and the doors inside stoved in. The cases had been broken open and rifled for gold and gems, and not readily tradeable objects were scattered around on the floor. The Leonardo bore the marks of a soldier's boot, but in spite of having been roughly handled, the other pictures showed no damage.

The Germans moved on, but by then the Soviet army was on the move from the east, and would be in Sieniawa in a matter of days. On 22 September Prince Augustyn turned up and removed the treasures to Pełkinie, the estate of his cousin Prince Witold Czartoryski, thereby effectively saving the collection from being seized by the Russians and sent east.

On 30 October Professor Komornicki was summoned by the Germans and on the next day left for Pełkinie with SS Stadartenführer Dr Kajetan Mühlmann, who had been appointed by Göring to investigate what was worth looting in Poland. On arrival, they were informed that the Gestapo had removed nine of the cases, including those containing the three masterpieces, and taken them to Rzeszów. The outraged Mühlmann called this 'looting' and set off with Komornicki for Rzeszów, where he duly reclaimed the case with the three masterpieces from the Gestapo and took it back to Kraków – but not to the Museum. Having served his purpose, Professor Komornicki was arrested and sent to the concentration camp at Sachsenhausen. On 25 January 1940 Mühlmann finalised his selection of 85 objects from the Czartoryski Museum to be taken to Germany, including pictures, illuminated manuscripts and examples of the decorative arts. But at this point the director of the Dresden *Gemäldegalerie*, the same Dr Posse who had attempted to delay the return of the Czartoryski items from Dresden in 1918, reappeared on the scene. He had now been appointed Hitler's plenipotentiary to loot in Poland, and he decided that the three Czartoryski masterpieces should form part of the Führer's own collection at Linz.

Prince Augustyn and Princess Dolores had been picked up by the Gestapo and repatriated to Spain in October, and responsibility for the Museum and its collections devolved onto Prince Witold Czartoryski, head of the *ordynacja* council. The Germans had requisitioned the Museum as soon as they entered Kraków and closed it to the public, but otherwise did not interfere. The personnel remained in place, but their salaries dwindled to symbolic levels; for patriotic reasons they refused to take the supplements

Prince Augustyn Czartoryski with his wife, Princess Dolores de Borbon-Orléans, and their son Adam Karol

offered by the German administration. They turned up for work as usual, but, as they had little to do, they began to play a part in the Polish resistance movement. The curiosities store-room became the meeting-place for the regional command of the underground Home Army. The department of paintings served as a store for the Army's pharmaceutical supplies, its archive was hidden on the same floor, and one ground-floor room was used as a meeting-point by the commander of the Kraków city division of the Home Army.

On 17 January 1945 the Germans evacuated Kraków, which was then occupied by Soviet troops. As peace settled on the country, Professor Stanisław Gąsiorowski, who had succeeded Komornicki in 1942, and his new assistant Marek Rostworowski waited to see how many of the looted treasures would find their way back.

The Leonardo, the Rembrandt and the Raphael had not remained in Berlin for long. They had taken the fancy of the brutal German governor of Poland and friend of Hitler, Dr Hans Frank, and sometime in 1943 he managed to get them back to Kraków, where

Professor Karol Estreicher surrounded by American soldiers recovering the *Lady with an Ermine* by Leonardo da Vinci in 1945

he hung them in his own apartments in the former castle of the Polish kings on Wawel hill. When he fled on 17 January 1945, he took them with him, first to Seichau in Silesia, and then to his villa at Schliersee near Neuhaus. It was there that he was arrested by the Americans on 4 May 1945. The Polish representative at the Allied commission for the retrieval of works of art, Professor Karol Estreicher, came to claim the stolen pictures on behalf of the Museum, but the Raphael 'Portrait of a Youth' was not among them.

When a full list of wartime losses was drawn up, it revealed that a total of 843 objects were missing, including fifteen paintings, twelve tapestries, 156 gold antiquities, 104 other gold objects, 64 royal memorabilia and 33 illuminated manuscripts. A few of these objects have found their way back to the Museum over the years, but there is still no trace of the Raphael.

Art and Politics

The feelings of relief at the end of the war were not to last, and sooner or later everyone in Poland had to confront the realities of life under Russian Communist rule. Institutions were no exception. The Czartoryski Museum had survived better than most, but its future remained unclear, and the family's hold over the institution was tenuous. On 1 July 1946 Prince Augustyn died of tuberculosis in Seville. The succession passed to Prince Adam Karol, born in Seville in 1940. The Polish courts appointed Prince Włodzimierz Czartoryski, son of Witold, who had died in 1945, curator of the child's inheritance. But the situation was anomalous.

The *ordynacja* had ceased to exist, abolished along with all other private institutions by decree of the Communist authorities. Sieniawa and its estate had been confiscated, but the properties in Kraków had not been affected, and the Museum drew a modest income from these. In the reduced circumstances, it was even necessary to rent out rooms on the first floor of the main building. The Museum, which had been qualified as an autonomous body by the Ministry of Culture, also received a small subsidy from it.

It was not long before the authorities began to take an unhealthy interest in the Museum. Marek Rostworowski was summoned to regional Party headquarters, where he was told that the Museum was 'a junk-heap', and that it was necessary to look back on the aristocratic past with the eyes of a peasant or a worker. Alarming rumours began to circulate that the Museum was going to be expropriated and nationalised. In the end the authorities decided to avoid such a blatant act of lawlessness. In December 1949 the Museum was taken into custody by the state and a year later incorporated into the National Museum in Kraków as a separate branch, the Czartoryski Collection, but without any formal act of expropriation.

The incorporation of the Czartoryski collections into the National Museum meant that far-reaching change was unavoidable. The Communist Party was determined that something be done to purge this 'ideologically jarring note' of an aristocratic, patriotic and cosmopolitan nature. Under Communism, culture had functions, the chief of which was the struggle against the class enemy. The intimate history of Poland's royal past was an affront to this struggle. Its message must be silenced, the *lacrimae rerum* noted by Virgil and quoted by Princess Izabela must be staunched.

Portrait of a young man by Raphael Santi, ca. 1510, looted by the Germans in 1939 and never recovered

The task was given to a curator recommended by the regional Party authorities, and he went about it with a will. He began with the picture gallery, where all the paintings were hung in a row. He then threw out all the nineteenth-century carved furniture. The crude new metal-and-glass showcases, painted a dispiriting grey, clashed with the exquisite exhibits. The accent was on grouping objects by function – clothes, arms, snuff-boxes. Thus the slippers of Madame de Maintenon, the pumps of Prince Adam Kazimierz Czartoryski and the crude boot lent to King Stanisław Augustus by one of his kidnappers were classified as 'lot of footwear, 16th to 18th centuries'. The Leonardo and the Rembrandt were moved to the National Museum in Warsaw; the archives to the state archives; the Polish archaeological finds to the Archaeological Museum; the royal regalia to the Wawel; musical instruments to the Museum of Musical Instruments in Poznań, and so on. And finally, there was a purge of the personnel, leaving only three of the staff in place.

It was not until the early 1960s that matters improved and some of the treasures were recovered. In 1965 Marek Rostworowski became director of the Czartoryski Collection branch of the National Museum in Kraków, and he began to reclaim the personality of the original museum through a complete rearrangement of the exposition. But major works were required in order to carry though this programme. The Palace was in such poor condition that collapse threatened. There was no proper security, fire precautions, air conditioning or modern lighting, no proper storage facilities or any ancillary arrangements.

The works began in 1970, and although a token exhibition of the treasures of the Collection was on view at the Arsenal, it was not until 1982 that it was possible to begin showing the Collection as a whole once again. The first to be installed were the Polish historical memorabilia and works of art. They were arranged in rooms which were themed according to kings or periods in a manner redolent of Princess Izabela's thinking. The socialist show-cases were discarded in favour of the old carved ones, which had fortunately survived, and many of the items removed in the 1950s and placed in other institutions were reclaimed.

The lack of clear definition of the Collection's ownership was a skeleton in the cupboard which haunted the thoughts of all concerned and conditioned their behaviour. It precluded the inclusion of any object from it in exhibitions that were to be sent abroad, in case this might be revindicated by the family. But there was no will to resolve the question, either by the family or by the government of the People's Republic of Poland. The former feared any move on their part might result in expropriation, the latter recoiled from anything that might provoke legal and diplomatic problems.

Princess Maria Ludwika had died in 1958, and the Hotel Lambert had been sold by her heirs in 1976. Her grandson Prince Adam Karol, brought up in Spain and England, knew little of Poland. But his first cousin and author of this book, a regular visitor to Poland from the late 1960s and in close touch with Marek Rostworowski, encouraged Prince Adam Karol to take an active interest and eventually brought the two together. Prince Adam Karol embraced the cause of Princess Izabela's legacy with enthusiasm. But all the ideas expressed then remained no more than pious hopes until 1989, when the realm of possibility was suddenly and dramatically expanded by the collapse of Communist power in Europe.

On 14 March 1991 the courts in Kraków confirmed Prince Adam Karol as the heir to his father's estate, and the Collection and the buildings it was housed in were recognized as being his property. At this crucial juncture, he acted with the selflessness characteristic of his forebears. He decided to guarantee the museum's future by giving it institutional status, while enshrining the link with the family, and on the advice of Marek Rostworowski, Professor Andrew Ciechanowiecki and the author, he decided to create a foundation which could own and administer it.

As things stood then, it was not possible for a totally autonomous institution to receive state funding, and the proposed foundation therefore had to affiliate itself to some state institution. The National Museum in Kraków, which currently administered the Collection, was the obvious choice, and matters were expedited by the fact that Marek Rostworowski had just been appointed deputy minister at the Ministry of Culture. On 23 September 1991 Prince Adam Karol signed a notarial act setting up the Foundation of the Princes Czartoryski at the National Museum of Kraków, to which he donated the Collection and the buildings in which it is housed. The state was represented

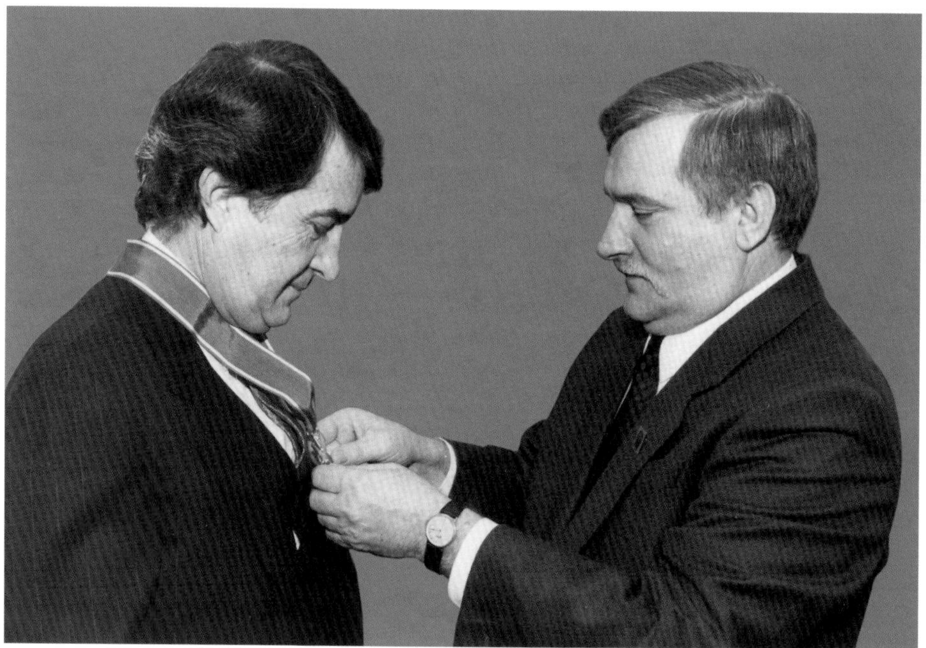

by the National Museum, whose director became *ex officio* chairman of the Foundation's board, and which continued to administer the Museum and Library. But the Founder himself retained extensive powers, and no less than five members of the family took their seats on the twelve-strong board.

One of the first major decisions to be taken by Prince Adam Karol in his new role was to give his assent to the loan of Leonardo's *Lady with an Ermine* to the National Gallery in Washington for the monumental exhibition *Circa 1492. Art in the Age of Exploration*. The National Museum in Kraków had been approached on the subject, but it had no power to give the assent, and this had led the matter to be raised by President George Bush himself with Lech Wałęsa during an official visit to Washington in April 1991. Having obliged both presidents by giving his assent, Prince Adam Karol was able to see the Czartoryski Museum take its place once more in the museum world through the loan of the picture, which took pride of place in the exhibition, and personally to represent both the Foundation and the President of Poland at the opening ceremonies.

Since 1991, the Foundation has managed to recover a magnificent 'polonaise' rug

Prince Adam Karol Czartoryski being decorated with the Order of Polonia Restituta by President Lech Wałęsa in 1991

stolen by the Germans during the war, and is attempting to revindicate various other items. There is still no trace of the Raphael, but the experience of history lends hope, for Princess Izabela's extraordinary creation has demonstrated a remarkable capacity for survival and regeneration.

More than any other private collection or bequest, however public-spirited and however philanthropic its patron, the concept given substance at Puławy sprang from a genuinely missionary passion. And this passion has consistently communicated itself to those who came into close contact with it. When disaster loomed in 1831, dozens of people came forward, willing to sacrifice not only their time and effort, but also their property and even their freedom in order to help preserve the treasures of Puławy. This devotion served the collection well over the next decades, with the result that by the time it opened in Kraków, it had not merely survived; it had gained in significance as a result of the effort and the sacrifice expended in its cause, and it was already well on the way to being a national institution. Throughout the dark days of the Second World War, people again risked their lives as well as their well-being in the cause of the Museum, and the struggle went on, underground, during the years of Communist rule.

Such a degree of devotion is hardly surprising, for the strange project that Princess Izabela launched at Puławy two centuries ago was not just some kind of Romantic *wunderkammer*. Nor was it merely a princely collection of fine art, of which there are so many. It was a great escapist dream trying to recapture an ideal past, both national and political, but also aesthetic and sentimental, and to project it as a wish for the future. It is a dream many can share.